ICE SCULPTURE

Secrets of a Japanese Master

Yukio Matsuo

John Wiley & Sons, Inc.
New York • Chichester • Brisbane • Toronto • Singapore

Shibata Edition Staff
Art Director: Hisao Isoda
Layout: Tomoko Amano
Editor: Atsue Suganuma
Illustration: Eiko Obata
Photography: Eiichi Takahashi
Cooperation: Takanawa Prince Hotel

Wiley Edition Staff
Senior Editor: Claire Thompson
Translator: Yoriko Powell
Managing Editor: Marcia Samuels
Production Coordinator: Christopher Lake, Publication Services, Inc.

Library of Congress Cataloging-in-Publication Data
Matsuo, Yukio
  [Hyōchōbi. English]
  Ice sculpture / Yukio Matsuo.
     p.   cm.
  Translation of: Hyōchōbi.
  ISBN 0-471-55409-X
     1. Matsuo, Yukio—Themes, motives. 2. Ice carving. I. Title.
  NK6030.M3813   1992
  736'.94—dc20   91-26696

Printed in Japan

10 9 8 7 6 5 4 3 2 1

FOREWORD

It was 12 years ago at the National Exhibition of Ice Sculpture. While waiting for the awards ceremony to begin after judging of the ice sculptures was finished, I looked around at all the works once again to confirm my grading of them. Since it was midsummer, the ice was melting rapidly and the shapes of the works had changed since they had been judged. Among the works changing shape, there was one sculpture that stood out conspicuously. At the time the works were judged it didn't attract attention, because it looked rough-hewn; however, it had come alive as time went by. This is the real ice sculpture, I thought. The essence of ice sculpture is to create them to show their best at the climax of events.

As a member of that judgment committee, I still feel ashamed that I couldn't foresee that this particular work was the real one. Ironically, the sculptor of the work was Mr. Yukio Matsuo, who now commands the authority of a consistently high-ranked prize winner who improved his skill while participating in many ice-sculpture contests.

I am very much pleased, from the bottom of my heart, that Yukio Matsuo is publishing a reference book on the ice sculpture of the new era based on his long experience on the subject. Although Japan is an advanced country in ice sculpture, only a few books on it have been published. I deeply hope that this one will usher in a new phase for this small group of reference books and that Matsuo's book will become a good friend of those young people who study ice sculpture.

Akira Kagajo
President, Japan Ice Carving Association

Matsuo, my colleague at the Takanawa Prince Hotel over many years, is undoubtedly the foremost artist working in the field of ice sculpture in Japan. Ice sculpture is a unique medium, one with many possibilities still undiscovered. This book will give ambitious young artists both guidance, through its instruction, and inspiration, by providing an opportunity to see the work of this master craftsman.

Seiroku Ogawa
Chef, Executive Director
Takanawa Prince Hotel

When I was a judge of the international cooking competition in Lyons, I unexpectedly came upon Matsuo demonstrating his magnificent ice sculpture technique. I have valued the role ice sculpture plays in banquets and other social occasions, and from this collection of works it is obvious to me that Matsuo has been breaking new ground in the field. I hope to see an increasing number of tasteful ice sculptures accentuating banquets as a result of the hints in this book.

Masakichi Ono
Chef, Executive Director, Hotel Okura

Create imaginary cathedrals, cradles, and sculptures from liquid and reflect imaginary lights. With a little water, construct a grotto of stalactites hanging in the sky and stalagmites rising to an unreal world. This is the miracle of Yukio Matsuo, a master of ice sculpture. And reading this beautiful book that describes the magnificent art of ice sculpture will bring it to each of us.

Writing in the eighteenth century, Antonin Carême predicted that for there to be masterpieces of gastronomy, books on cooking and confectionery were needed. In this book, Matsuo provides the same inspiration. Bringing to others beauty thus visualized and defined is indeed a prelude to feasts.

Michel Malapris
President, French Culinary Academy

We had opportunities to visit many foreign countries in the world, European countries and Canada as well as Japan. And in all of those countries you showed us the wonderful world of ice sculpture. We, all of us in the World Steward League, would like to express our thanks to you for that. I am sure that this book will be very useful to everyone who has it in their hands.

Hans Bushkens
Chairman, World Steward League

I am happy to have this opportunity to write a foreword for this beautiful book. I know Yukio Matsuo—a chef as well as an ice sculptor—very well, and I am impressed by his work. He can create with splendid swiftness and accuracy a motif that bears comparison with crystal.

Although the culinary world is full of frequent change, with many big waves, there is nothing but admiration when the cuisine is arranged beautifully, with the delicious taste suitable to the arrangement, and accompanied by works designed and sculpted by Matsuo.

Roger Roucou
Owner and Chef, Restaurant La Mère Guy

Yukio Matsuo shows his works in a first-class hotel in Paris every year. Giving full play to his talent in ice sculpture, he always achieves a great success. Works by this artist, who is also my friend, attain the level of perfection. Although his works are short-lived because the material is ice, they yield to none of the greatest sculptures of the past. Whenever I come upon his works, I am always captivated by the quickness with which he produces them and the elaborateness of detail; I cannot help admiring them. Using this space, I would like to offer my sincere applause to Mr. Matsuo.

Jean-Jacques Barbier
Chef de Cuisine, Hôtel Intercontinental, Paris

For my friend, Yukio Matsuo, of the Takanawa Prince Hotel: When an artist such as you brings your hand with a chisel down on a block of ice, pieces fly around and in the twinkling of an eye something unexpected comes into being. It is very delightful to see what only the artist himself knew was going to be completed.

The finished work is not only superior to the motif itself, with brilliant magnificence like diamonds, but, with a sense of harmony, the works connect sculptural art with epicurism. What a joy it is!

Guy Legay
Chef de Cuisine, Hôtel Ritz

The Chinese had a strong interest in using ice several centuries ago not only for transportation and preservation of food but as a decoration for cuisine to delight diners at banquets.

Placing slices of fish or even whole fishes on platforms made of ice and works carved in big blocks of ice enhanced the value of the food served. It emphasized the freshness of the food, and feasted guests' eyes as well as stimulating the taste buds. And it was effective in tempting the appetite. For the past 25 years, the Japanese have been successfully tackling ice with chisel in hand, using a new method. They make vivid works using oblique and sharp lines like diamond facets, not the round outlines of before. Several hours after completion, the sharp edges of the works start to gain roundness and the works lose their shine, change shape. Then they gradually lose their lives, and eventually they disappear. We could say that this is the fate of beautiful things.

When I turn back to Yukio Matsuo, an artist and also my friend, I find him already forgetting about dying work, facing a new block of ice with chisels in each hand, and scattering chips of ice. To captivate us again, he is trying to blow several hours of life into ice anew.

Andri Tiefault
President and Founder
l'Amicale des Cuisiniers et Pâtissiens Français Japon

Yukio Matsuo splendidly expresses the transparency of crystals, vortexes, and soaring with only a chisel—which in the arts belongs in the realm of sculpture.

Rodin of the North Pole breaks ice and blows a warm look into ice. He continues to carve work with short lives for a long time to give us the joy of seeing them.

I wish this artist great success and I want to praise his works.

Pierre Troisgros
Owner, Chef, Restaurant-Hôtel Troisgros

PREFACE

Three years after I started work as a cook, I encountered a swan at a banquet: this was my first sight of ice sculpture. Since I was born in Hokkaido, I was familiar with ice; also, I liked to draw. So I jumped at ice sculpture and carved in my own way, using carpenter's chisels. However, it didn't turn out as I wished. One day, after continued trial and failure, I saw an ice sculpture 3 meters high (whose title I've forgotten), and I was greatly impressed with the beauty and drama of it. That experience was the start of my learning about ice sculpture in earnest. I think it was about 15 years ago that I finally developed my own style, after hard study on my own and under the late Hideo Kubodera.

This book contains the results of my education to date. In it I introduce many of my own ideas—the use of gouge chisels, for example, and how to decorate with lights and flowers. I hope that my book will serve as a reference and guide for others in creating ice sculpture.

For the opportunity to devote myself to ice sculpture in this way I am indebted to the Takanawa Prince Hotel and their ice sculpture department, and I thank them.

Yukio Matsuo

CONTENTS

PART 1

Collection of Works

The South Pole
explanation page 126

The South Pole

explanation page 126

Loneliness at the Lakeside
explanation page 127

Imitator

explanation page 128

Fighting Cock
explanation page 129

18

Pigeon on the World
explanation page 130

19

Migration

explanation page 131

Lord of the Sky
explanation page 132

Master of the Woods
explanation page 133

Honey Collectors
explanation page 133

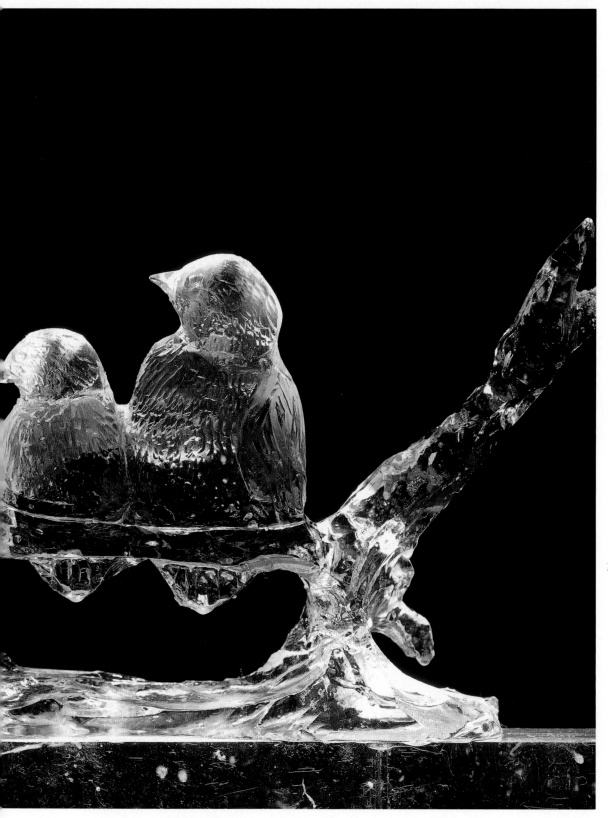

Love
explanation page 136

24

Eagles
explanation page 134

His Majesty
explanation page 137

Autumn Poem
explanation page 138

Citizens of the Ocean
explanation page 139

Joyful Summer Memory
explanation page 140

Dancing *Ayu*
explanation page 141

Time of the Angelfish
explanation page 142

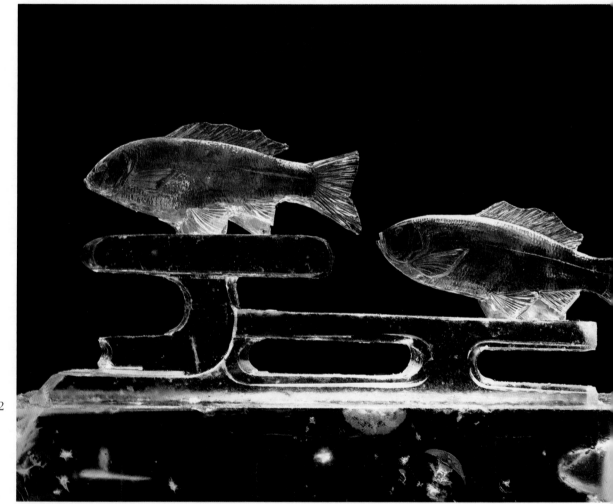

Endeavor
explanation page 143

33

Noble Seahorse
explanation page 144

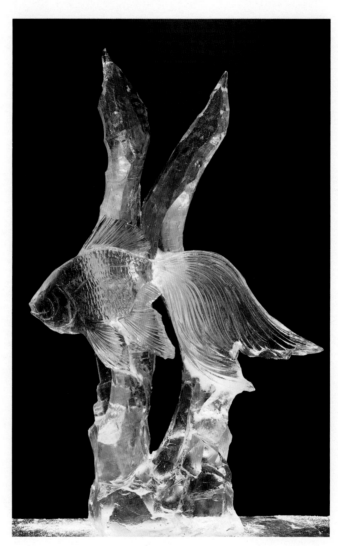

Floating Amber
explanation page 144

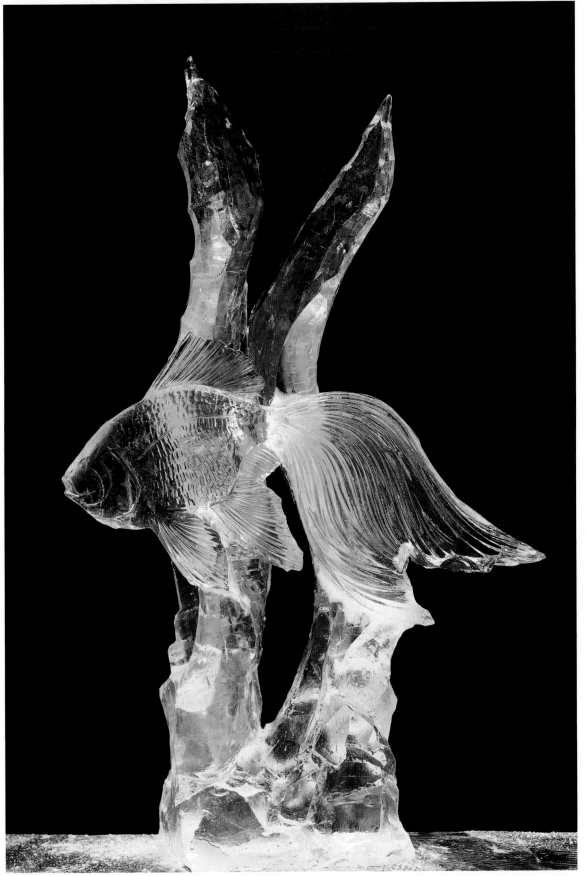

Jump for Joy

explanation page 145

Angel's Chair
explanation page 146

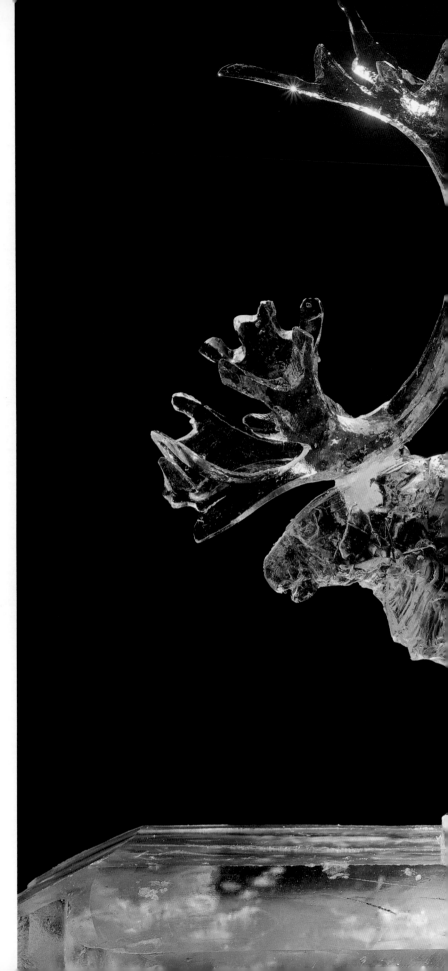

Traveler in the Snow
explanation page 147

My Way
explanation page 146

Over the Horizon

explanation page 148

Relief C
explanation page 149

Cinderella
explanation page 150

Heartstrings
explanation page 151

Frozen Jade
explanation page 152

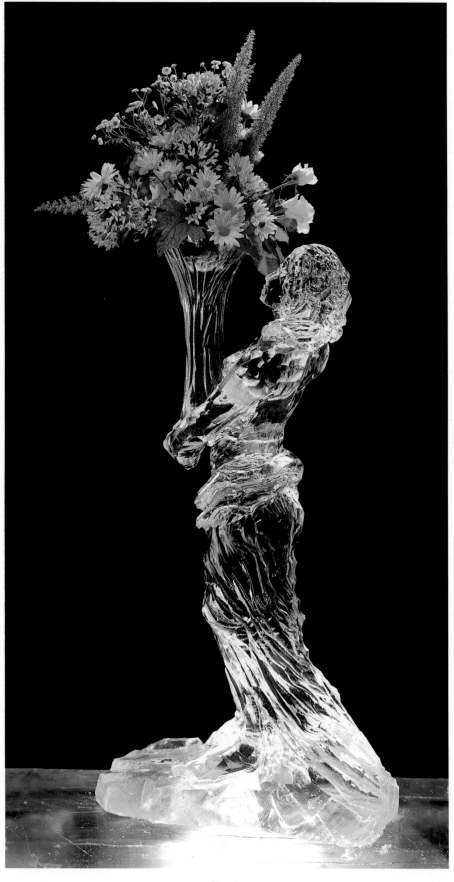

Beauty
explanation page 150

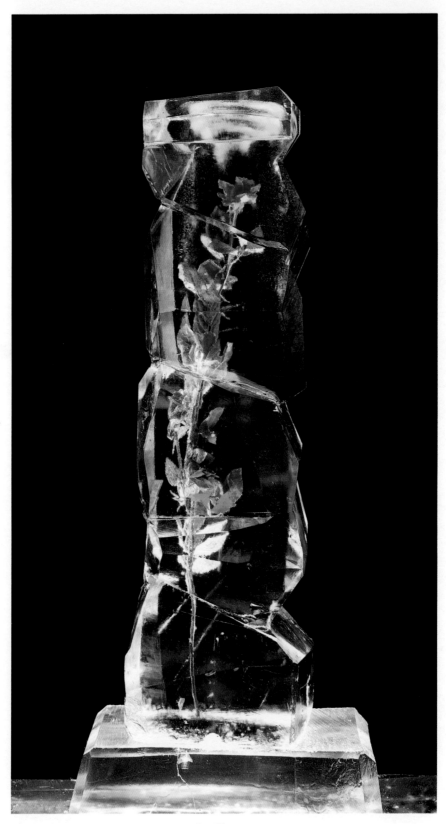

Ice Flower

explanation page 153

Ice Flower

explanation page 153

Royal Carriage
explanation page 154

Spring Swans
explanation page 155

Ice and Flower Monuments
explanation page 156

Simplicity
explanation page 157

Glass within a Glass
explanation page 157

Predator

explanation page 158

Splash

explanation page 159

57

Snow House
explanation page 159

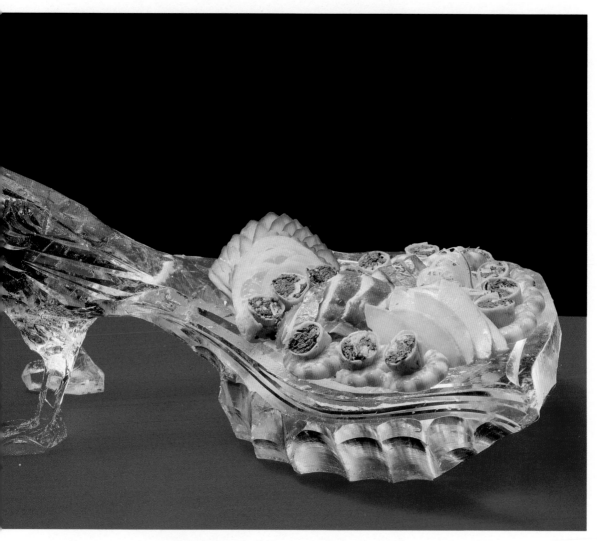

Proud Peacock

explanation page 160

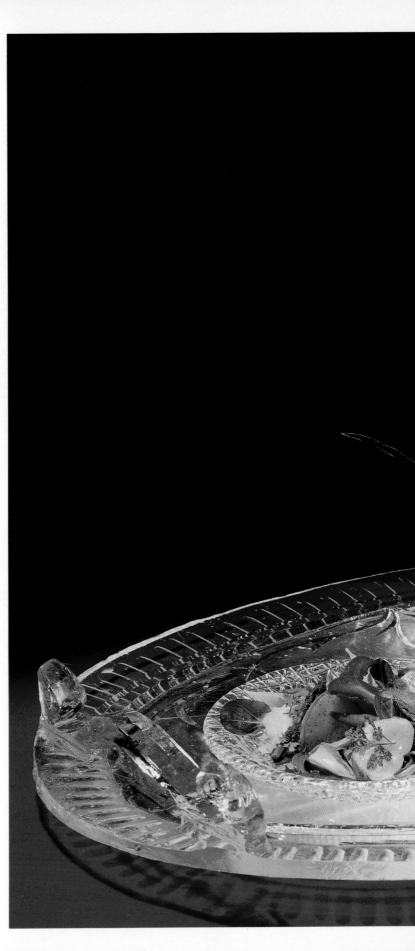

Lobster
explanation page 161

60

The Winner
explanation page 162

Delicious
explanation page 162

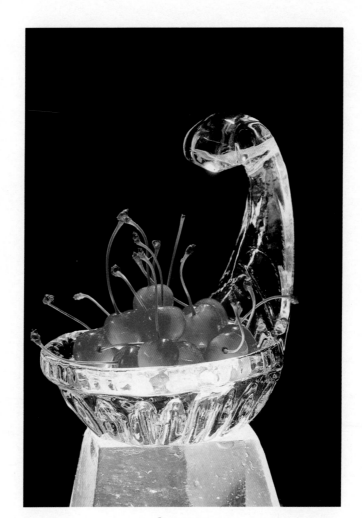

Sweetness
explanation page 160

Drive around the Blue Lagoon
explanation page 165

Melody of Love
explanation page 164

68

T. Kasai, *Kencho*
explanation page 165

A. Poncet, *Fugue Expand*
explanation page 165

Howling Wind
explanation page 166

Triangle of Hope
explanation page 166

Birds of the South Wind

explanation page 167

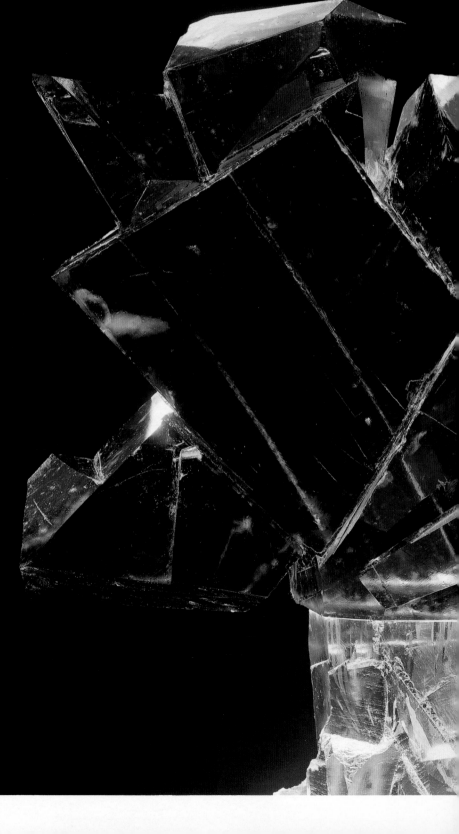

73

G.Sugimoto *The Earth*
explanation page 167

K.Akaogi *Stripe Arch*
explanation page 168

75

Flowery Flakes of Snow
explanation page 169

Swan Trio
explanation page 168

A. Archipenko, *Standing Nude II*
explanation page 170

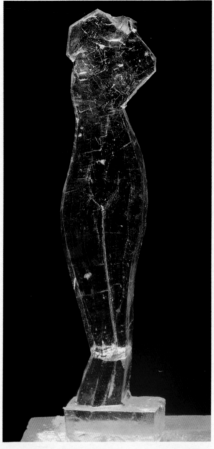

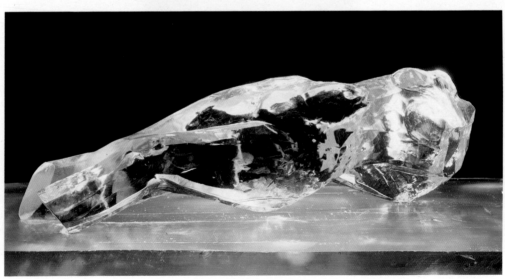

Blooming Woman
explanation page 170

O. Zadkine Sculpture

explanation page 169

Peacock's Spring Light
explanation page 171

80

Seahorses in the Spring Water of Apollon
explanation page 172

Aurora

explanation page 173

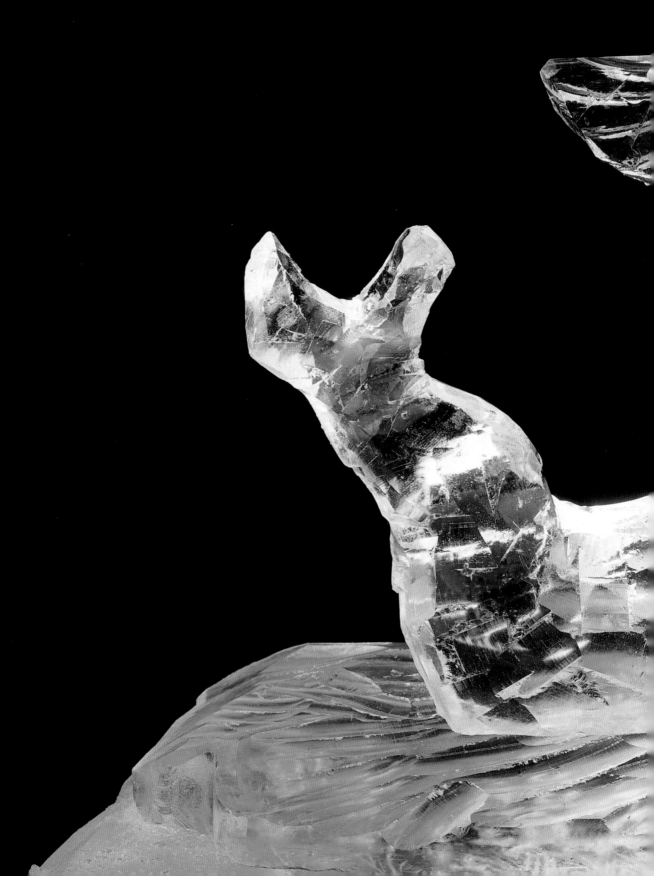

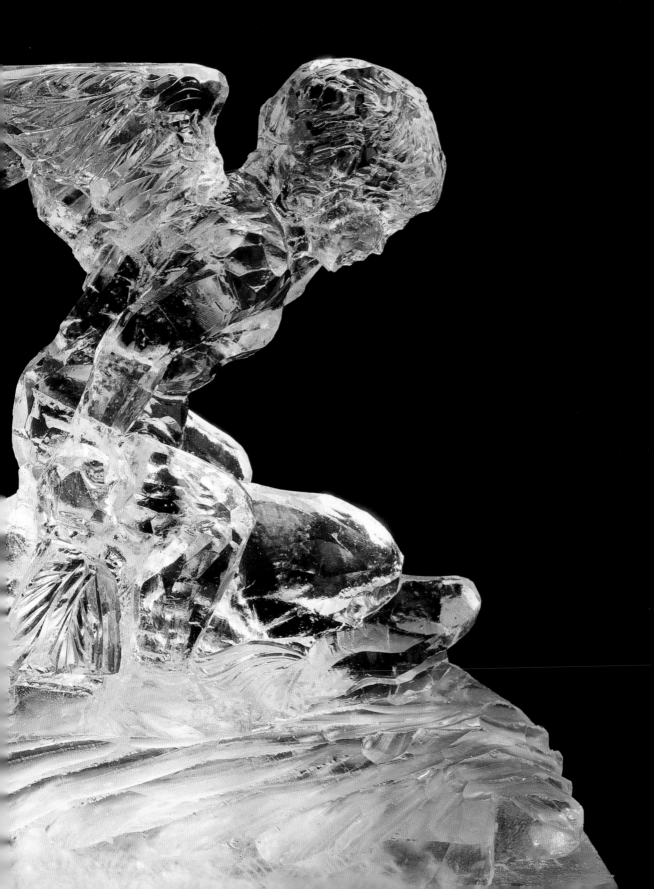

Head

Ben Hur
(from front)

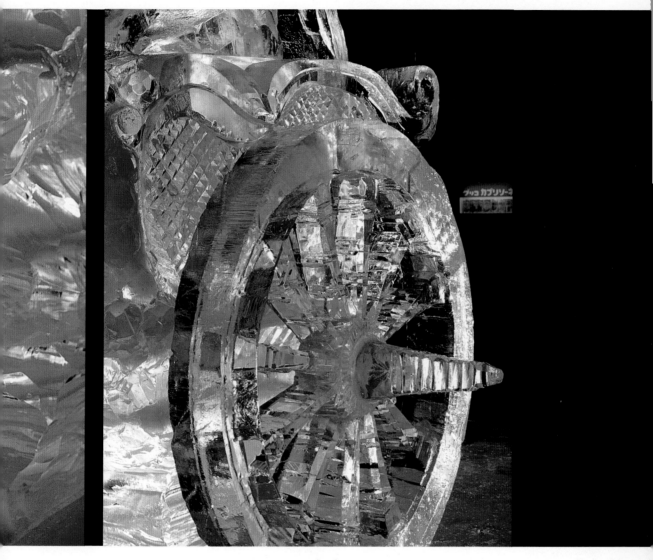

Wheel   93

Ben Hur
(from rear)

A Flock of Reindeer
explanation page 174

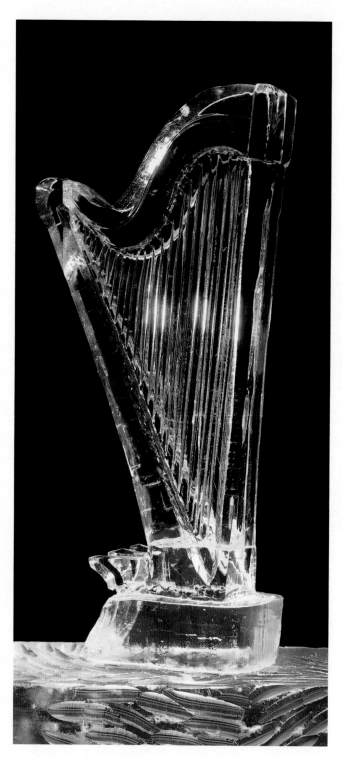

Silver Harp
explanation page 175

Twilight
explanation page 176

98

Eiffel Tower
explanation page 177

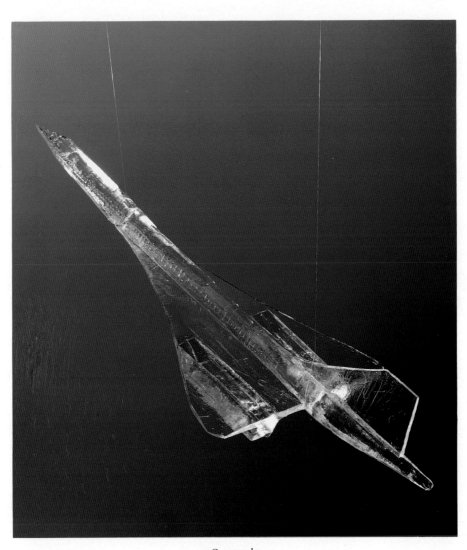

Concorde

explanation page 178

Brontosaurus
explanation page 179

Congratulations
(Calligraphic Chinese
Character *Kotobuki*)
explanation page 179

Merry Christmas
explanation page 179

Collection of Works

For Reference

Collected works, mainly party decorations for events between 1974 and 1987. The dates of production are listed in parentheses.

* 1

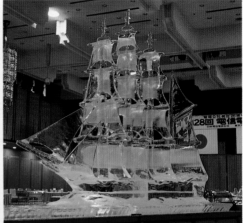

* 2

* 1 Sailing vessel. It is 3 meters high and 3.5 meters wide. The sails on the masts are important. They are made to look like fabric by using the opaque parts of the ice. The picture is the vessel shining in the sunset, using orange and blue lighting. The right photograph was taken five hours after the sculpture was set out; it still retains total balance. (October 2, 1977)

* 2 The sailing vessel in * 1 recreated and set in a pond. When lit with a spotlight, the sculpture gives off a luster and a unique atmosphere. (December 23, 1977)

* 4

* 3 The crane on the left is made from a single block
of ice, with wings, torso, and legs carved
separately, a method that uses ice economically.
The important feature is the balance between
each part. (December 4, 1974)

* 4 For the welcome party at the World Cup Skiing
Championship series. Eagles were chosen as a
theme to give the feeling of soaring. In the
Championship, young athletes from all over the
world pit their technique against each other.
(February 22, 1977)

* 6

* 5 A Chinese phoenix displayed at a celebratory banquet. The cross section of the tail is carved in an L-shape to reduce the weight of the tail so that it can survive for several hours. (July 3, 1975)

* 6 A Chinese phoenix carved in the same way as *5, with a slightly different style. (December 5, 1976)

* 7

108

* 7 A pair of swans carved life-size. When creating a
pair, it makes good, balanced composition to
carve the wings of one swan open and the wings
of the other closed. (April 8, 1981)

* 9

* 8 Flowers in ice. These are used as focal points for
     desserts. Both are 30 centimeters high. (July 2,
     1981)

* 9 A flower vase made as a small carriage. A display
     for a small banquet. (September 7, 1983)

* 10

110

* 10 Every Christmas Eve, a large sculpture suitable
for the hotel garden is developed; evergreen
trees strung with lights serve as background.
  This work depicts reindeer and an angel playing
a heart-shaped harp and it measures 3.5 meters
high and 15 meters wide, 100 ice blocks were
used in its constuction. (December 24, 1982)

* 11 Snapshots taken on Christmas Eve (bottom) and
the next morning (top). This design took into
consideration the work's contrast with the winter
camellias blossoming in the garden. (December
24, 1982)

* 11

112

* 12

* 12   A pair of mated hawks. Hawks are the motif that
       I create best. Emphasize the facial   expressions
       and the sharp tails. (September 7, 1984)

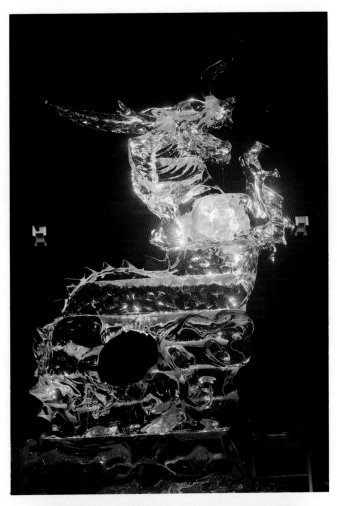

* 13

* 13 On the left and right are rising dragons. It is im-
        portant to express volume and force by carving
        the dragons rough. (June 19, 1981)

 14

* 15

* 14 A display at a party for introducing new products for a ski manufacturer. Combining a set of real skis and poles with the sculpture resulted in a stirring pose that highlighted the sponsor's equipment. (March 20, 1981)

* 15 A display for an event at a restaurant. To best present the work, I lighted the sculpture to project its silhouette. (February 14, 1981)

* 16

* 17

* 16 A fruit display with a motif of a woman wearing a
dress. For the lengthy banquet, the whole thing
was carved roughly, but with emphasis on the
feautures of the face and the lines of the dress.
(December 17, 1981)

* 17 For a welcome party for an American football
team, a figure passing a football was created. The
team's logo was embedded between slabs of ice
to make a focal point at the feet. (January 12,
1982)

* 18

* 18 This sculpture is a woman supporting the sponsor's trademark on her right hand. The display includes pink roses. The composition is simple, but the work exemplifies the basics of carving the human body. (June 2, 1984)

* 19

117

* 19 This powerful 2.5-meter-high work is suitable for
a New Yokozuna's complete victory commem-
orative party. The *shide* (the apronlike zigzag
shapes hanging from the figure's waist) is carved
deeply and stuffed with snow to bring the area
into relief. (September 3, 1979)

* 21

* 20

* 20   A *kabuto* (traditional Japanese helmet) displayed
       on the occasion of Boys' Festival. Yellow lighting
       cast on the 1-meter-long hoe-shaped helmet crest
       dramatizes the bravery of a *Sengoku* samurai.
       (February 12, 1981)

* 21   A five-story pagoda with a pair of guardian dogs,
       one on each side. When setting the work on a
       table, it is important to adjust the height of each
       roof. (October 25, 1980)

＊ 22

＊ 22 A 2.5-meter-high, 3.6-meter-wide palanquin
created for a party attended mostly by foreign
guests. Each person carrying the palanquin is in a
different pose. Their high spirits are emphasized
through the movement suggested by their legs.
(October 18, 1979)

* 23

* 23 A six-horse carriage suitable for the occasion (a
      wedding reception), and carved to be harmon-
      ious with the large banquet space. Forty trans-
      parent ice blocks were used. (July 12, 1985)

* 25

* 24 A castle and a carriage carved using 200 blocks
      of ice. A fantastic image floating in the dark was
      expressed by placing ten lights inside the castle
      and six lights behind it. (December 24, 1983)

* 25 For a wedding reception to take place in a hotel
      garden, the theme is the couple's future home,
      New York City. At 4 meters high and 7 meters
      wide, it used 70 blocks of ice. (June 12, 1987)

* 27

* 26 This statue of Joan of Arc was created for a
      Bastille Day entertainment held by the restaurant
      Trianon in the Takanawa Prince Hotel. (July 14,
      1981)

* 27 The logo of a sponsor. Harmony was achieved
      with light and water by setting the sculpture in
      the water and illuminating it. (June 4, 1985)

* 29

* 28 This decoration, featuring flowers cascading out of a block of ice, graced the cocktail lounge before a dinner show. (April 24, 1983)

* 29 A production for the toast at a wedding reception. The base of a cannon was carved in ice and a champagne bottle was placed on it. (February 11, 1985)

124

* 30

* 30 A treasure ship with a Chinese phoenix prow,
suitable for a New Year's banquet. The sponsor's
logo is inserted in the sail. The piece is 2.5
meters high and 4 meters wide, built from 16
blocks of ice. (January 16, 1985)

Explanation of the Works

Color photographs on pages 13 and 14.

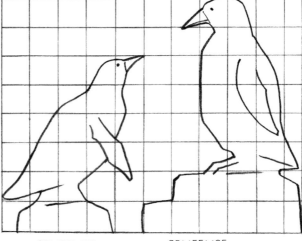

60×50×25   80×55×25

To achieve a childlike look, casually carve the whole body of the baby penguin with the front side of a flat chisel. This method also will make the sculpture survive longer.

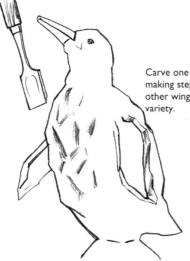

Carve one of the wings in relief, making steps on it, and carve the other wing extended forward for variety.

Score grooves for eye sockets with a "V" angle chisel (wedge) chisel and bore the edge with a pointed knife. Then stuff the eyes with snow to highlight them. Snow can be collected when you shave the ice with an electric saw.

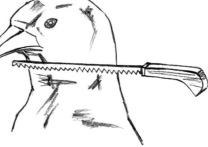

126

Make the beaks thick and avoid making the beak tips sharp. This technique is important not only for carving penguins, but for any kind of bird, because thicker sculptures keep longer.

When carving places where it is difficult to fit a chisel, such as under the penguin's bill, use a fret or scroll saw. The same applies to carving other kinds of sculptures.

Parent and baby penguins: Their bodies have no defined waists, they have short legs, and their wings have fins. Carve the adult penguin with a smooth surface, but when carving the baby, leave traces of chisel marks to express its youth.

Color photograph on page 15.

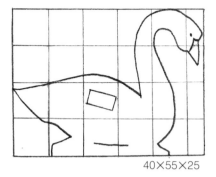

40×55×25

55×40×25

Score grooves on the swan's wings using a "V" angle (wedge) chisel at a slant, to show how the feathers are piled up. Two wings are needed, but make only one template and reverse it to make the other wing. (The measurements here are for only one wing.)

Use the front side of the flat chisel to carve two surfaces which flow from the top of the head to the back, beginning halfway from the top of the head, down to the center of neck. Then reverse the flat chisel and use the back of it to carve from around the center of the neck to the swan's back.

Carve the sockets for the wings a little larger than the size of the notch on the wings. After placing the wings in position, stuff snow in the space between the wings and the body to glue them together. It is important to attach the wings one by one after putting the body on the stand, and to join the ice using a saw to fix the wings firmly. (Note: An explanation of joining ice pieces using a saw is on page 189.)

Carve two surfaces from under the chin to the stomach using the back side of a flat chisel. Cut in an upward stroke from the stomach to the chin. Use a scroll saw to carve curves where it is difficult to put the chisel.

127

Corner

The swan opens its wings and casts down its eyes, showing elegance. The neck line is the especially important feature. Carve a beautiful, curving line to make the cross-section lozenge-shaped. Although it requires a good command of the use of the front and back sides of a chisel, this technique enables sculptures to last longer and to gain more beautifully flowing lines as time passes.

IMITATOR

Color photograph on page 16.

Make the beak and the crest thick.
Sweep the crest upward.

40×40×25

Roughly carve folded wings with a
"V" angle (wedge) chisel, stroking
along the body in one direction.
Use a gouge chisel to carve the
feathers on the chest. To make the
perch look like a tree trunk, shave
it with bold strokes.

128

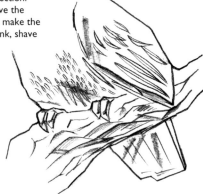

Two toes extend forward when the
bird sits on a perch.

Parrots have characteristic feather crests behind their heads and big,
short beaks whose tips curve downward. Accordingly, emphasize these
characteristics; also pay attention to the compositional balance with the
perch.

FIGHTING COCK

Color photograph on page 17.

Make the cockscomb thick: shave it with large strokes, using the back side of a flat chisel, as if scooping it.

With a "V" angle (wedge) chisel, score grooves around the eyes to make them sharp, deep, and rugged.

60×55×25

First shave off the excess ice with a saw. Then carve roughly with the front side of a flat chisel, and make the outline with a gouge chisel. Carve the tail as if it is floating, and make the unevenness of the neck and chest feathers clear. Move the chisels with quick, decisive strokes.

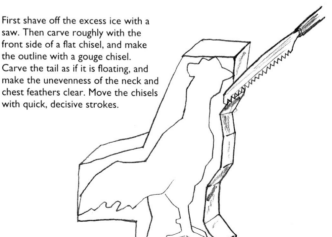

129

Leave the ice between the feet for support. Make the toes stand out clearly in relief.

A fighting gamecock. Express its courage by tilting the face upward and sharpening the beak and eyes. Although the neck is long and thin, the feathers around it rise softly when the bird gets excited. Express this feature using a gouge chisel.

Color photograph on page 18.

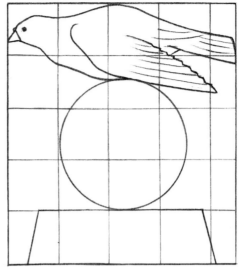

Pigeon 15 x 45 x 27
Ball   25 x 25 x 25
Stand 10 x 37 x 20

The bumps over the beak are one of the pigeon's distinctive features. Carve the eyes using the same method as when carving penguins.

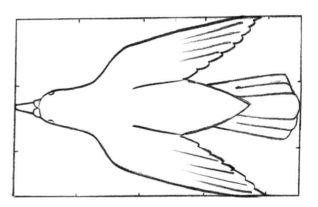

View from above: A pigeon flying forward. The sense of speed is shown by the openness of the flight feathers and the way the tail feathers close.

130

Sharply and deeply groove the wing feathers with a "V" angle (wedge) chisel at an angle a little bit toward the right and toward the ends of the feathers. Make the tips of the feathers in the shape of a mountain.

A composition combining a pigeon flying through the air and a ball. To connect the pigeon and the ball, make a depression in the chest of the pigeon to fit with the curvature of the ball, and glue them together with snow. Refer to page 190 for the method of carving balls.

Color photograph on page 19.

60×50×25

Back view: It is important to make the reeds thick to support the flying duck. To balance the composition, carve the duck connected to the reeds from the center of its back to its tail.

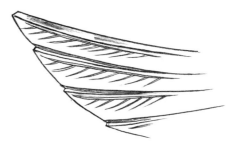

Highlight the border between the beak and face with a "V" angle (wedge) chisel, and with a flat chisel, carve a step to make the beak surface lower than the face surface.

Groove the flight feathers deep and sharp with a "V" angle (wedge) chisel to express the strength of the beating wings. Groove the lines of the feathers with the same chisel.

131

Make a bulge at the chin.

To create a realistic duck, take note of the animal's habit of taking flight vertically from the surface of the water. This sculpture captures such a scene, at a moment when a duck flaps its wings, pushing them forward. Note particularly the space between the wings and the splashing water surface.

LORD OF THE SKY

Color photograph on page 20.

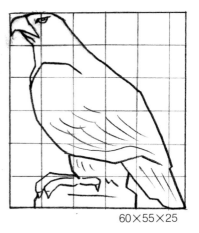

Make this part thick.

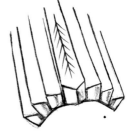

60×55×25

The eyes are stern and the beak is large and sharp. Carve the line of feathers from the head to the neck along the body line with a gouge chisel.

Score the line of feathers on the breast area dynamically, from the top to the bottom. Firmly hold a "V" angle (wedge) chisel at 60 degrees to the chest area, and score vigorously to create variety in level; leave a trace of edge to make the roughness visible.

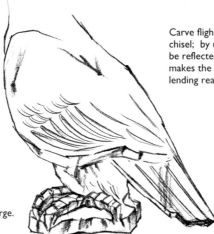

Carve flight feathers with a gouge chisel; by using this chisel, light can be reflected in a unique way that makes the feathers look glossy, lending reality to the figure.

132

Carve three talons, rough and large.

Score the line of tail feathers with a "V" angle (wedge) chisel.

The distinctive features of eagles are their sharp beaks, sharp wings, and strong feet. Because it is difficult to maintain balance in a composition with closed wings, it is important to occasionally stand back from the work to check the overall balance.

MASTER OF THE WOODS

Color photograph on page 21.

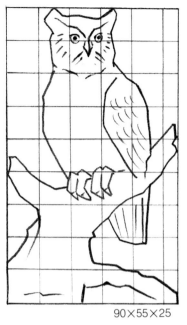

Bulge the area around the chin.

Roughly shave the body with the front side of a flat chisel. Then carve the line of feathers on the chest, head, and face, along the body line, with a gouge chisel. Carve the line of feathers on the chest in the same way as when carving an eagle.

90×55×25

Striped owls have large heads and flat faces. Their characteristic features are feather tufts that look like ears, round eyes, sharp beaks, and fat, large claws.

HONEY COLLECTORS

Color photograph on page 22.

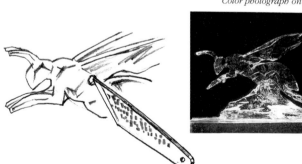

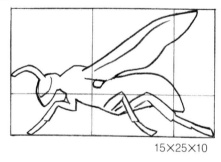

133

Hollow a hole with the tip of a pointed knife.

15×25×10

Carve antennae, head, body, wings, and legs of bees rather thick. For such a small work as this, work on Styrofoam board and carve carefully in detail. Use a pointed knife, scroll saw, and wood-carving chisel.

EAGLES

Color photograph on page 24.

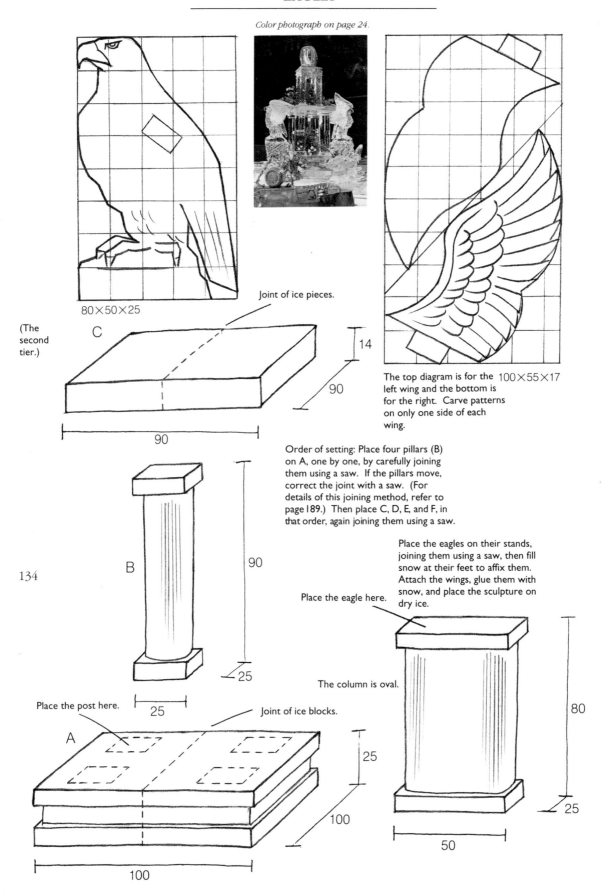

80×50×25

(The second tier.)

Joint of ice pieces.

C

90

90

14

90

The top diagram is for the 100×55×17 left wing and the bottom is for the right. Carve patterns on only one side of each wing.

Order of setting: Place four pillars (B) on A, one by one, by carefully joining them using a saw. If the pillars move, correct the joint with a saw. (For details of this joining method, refer to page 189.) Then place C, D, E, and F, in that order, again joining them using a saw.

134

B

90

25

25

Place the eagle here.

Place the eagles on their stands, joining them using a saw, then fill snow at their feet to affix them. Attach the wings, glue them with snow, and place the sculpture on dry ice.

The column is oval.

Place the post here.

A

Joint of ice blocks.

25

100

100

100

80

50

25

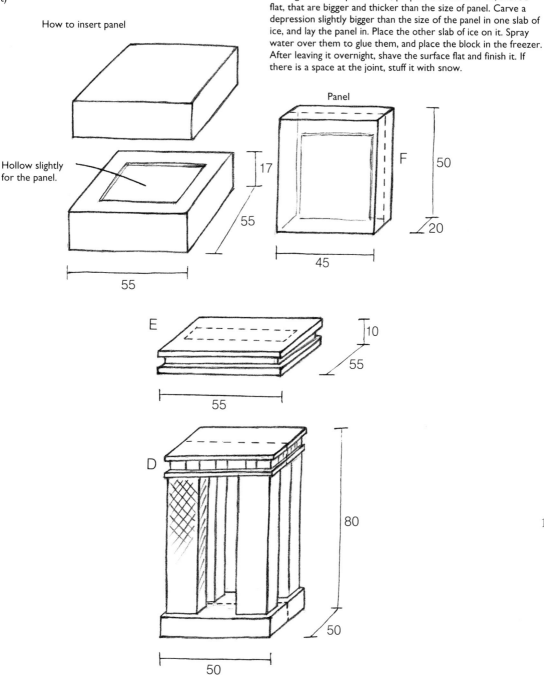

How to insert panel

Making the insert panel: First, prepare two slabs of ice, shaved flat, that are bigger and thicker than the size of panel. Carve a depression slightly bigger than the size of the panel in one slab of ice, and lay the panel in. Place the other slab of ice on it. Spray water over them to glue them, and place the block in the freezer. After leaving it overnight, shave the surface flat and finish it. If there is a space at the joint, stuff it with snow.

Hollow slightly for the panel.

Panel

55

17

55

F

50

45

20

E

10

55

55

D

80

50

50

135

Displayed eagles with a panel sandwiched between ice slabs. It is very important to carve the stand carefully, record the sizes of each part, set it up in the correct order, and thoroughly join the parts with a saw. When there are gaps left after joining the parts, stuff the space with snow. The method of carving the eagles is the same as explained on page 132.

LOVE

Color photograph on page 23.

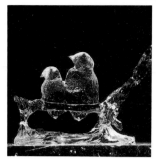

30×40×17

Based on the sketch, rough out the form with a saw and a flat chisel.

After finishing 80 percent of the top part, use a flat chisel to make the empty space under the branch. Carve the refined lines using a scroll saw and a pointed knife. Score the feathers with a gouge chisel and the wings with a "V" angle (wedge) chisel.

The combination of two small birds makes for a warm atmosphere. For expressiveness, turn both faces in the same direction, aiming their gazes high and low.

HIS MAJESTY

Color photograph on page 25.

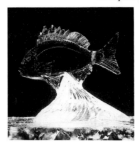

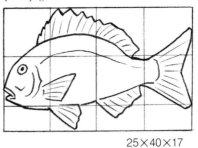

$25 \times 40 \times 17$

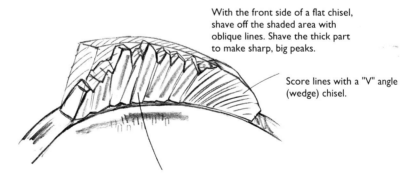

Slightly jut out.

Score the line with a "V" angle (wedge) chisel.

Place the fish on the stand and glue them together with snow.

With the front side of a flat chisel, shave off the shaded area with oblique lines. Shave the thick part to make sharp, big peaks.

Score lines with a "V" angle (wedge) chisel.

For roughness, make indentations with a flat chisel, and give the impression of the joint between bones and dorsal fin.

From the mouth to the dorsal fin, a sea bream is roundish, and the area above the eyes protrudes slightly. The dorsal and tail fins are bony. It is best to emphasize these characteristics.

AUTUMN POEM

Color photograph on page 26.

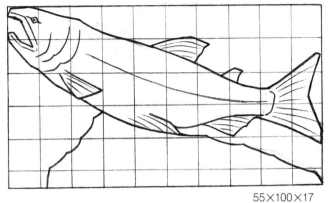

55×100×17

Shave with the front side of a flat
chisel and show the thickness.

Include the soft dorsal fin characteristic
of the salmon family.

Score lines with a "V" angle
(wedge) chisel.

Score the lines of the flap that
protects the gills with a "V" angle
(wedge) chisel. Then carve gills in
layers with a flat chisel.

138

Bulge this area.

Carve the stand with a gouge chisel,
using large sweeps to make it look
as if waves are swaying.

It is good to use a twisting body and opening mouth to express the
salmon's effort to swim upstream to spawn. The lines of the back and
the fins should be thick. After scoring the lateral line on the side of the
salmon with a "V" angle (wedge) chisel, systematically score scales
from top to bottom with a gouge chisel. Make the form lines clear with
the chisel. These carving techniques are common to sculpting any kind
of fish.

Color photograph on page 27.

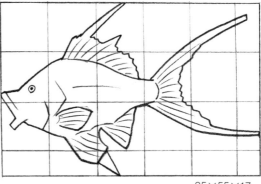

35×55×17

These areas need to be shaved away.

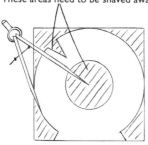

Accurately draw a 25-cm diameter circle and a 10-cm diameter circle using a compass. Shave out the inner area, and remove a triangular area with oblique lines for inserting the ventral fin.

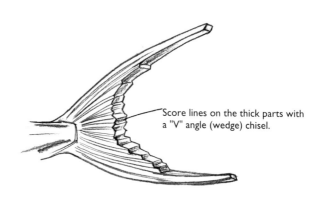

Score lines on the thick parts with a "V" angle (wedge) chisel.

139

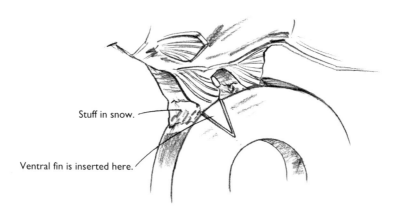

Stuff in snow.

Ventral fin is inserted here.

Characteristics of the Sakura sea bream are similar to those of the sea bream on page 137, except the top and bottom parts of its tail fin are long. Make the fish lively by opening its mouth and scoring lines on the upper and lower lips for definition.

Color photograph on page 28.

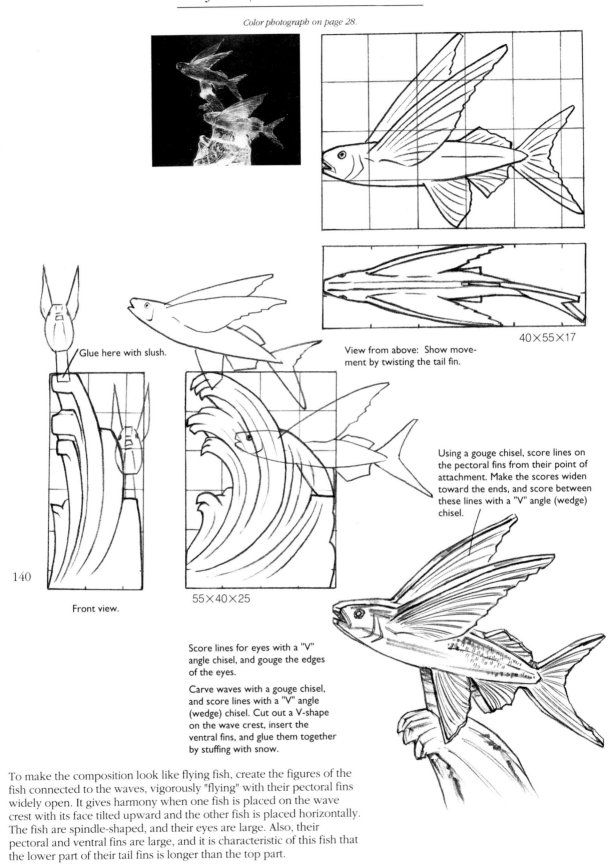

40×55×17

Glue here with slush.

View from above: Show movement by twisting the tail fin.

Front view.

55×40×25

Using a gouge chisel, score lines on the pectoral fins from their point of attachment. Make the scores widen toward the ends, and score between these lines with a "V" angle (wedge) chisel.

Score lines for eyes with a "V" angle chisel, and gouge the edges of the eyes.

Carve waves with a gouge chisel, and score lines with a "V" angle (wedge) chisel. Cut out a V-shape on the wave crest, insert the ventral fins, and glue them together by stuffing with snow.

To make the composition look like flying fish, create the figures of the fish connected to the waves, vigorously "flying" with their pectoral fins widely open. It gives harmony when one fish is placed on the wave crest with its face tilted upward and the other fish is placed horizontally. The fish are spindle-shaped, and their eyes are large. Also, their pectoral and ventral fins are large, and it is characteristic of this fish that the lower part of their tail fins is longer than the top part.

140

Color photograph on page 30.

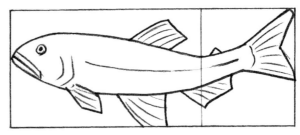

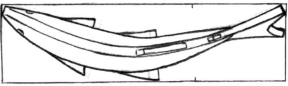

View from above: The key feature is
the way the body is twisted.

6×15×4

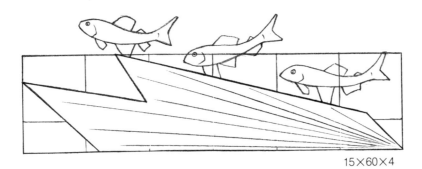

15×60×4

Maintain thickness in this part.

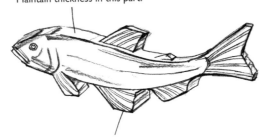

Make the bottom part of the ventral
fin flat, and put the fish on the
stand; glue them together with
snow that is just barely slushy.

Draw the bottom diagram of the *ayu* with a streamlined shape swimming
up a clear stream. Be especially careful with the twist of the bodies and
the way their tail fins sweep upward. The atmosphere of a clear stream
can be created by vigorously carving the stand in long strokes with a "V"
angle (wedge) chisel.

Color photograph on page 32.

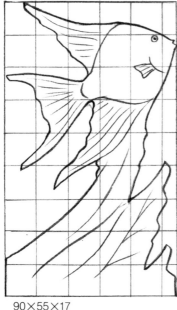

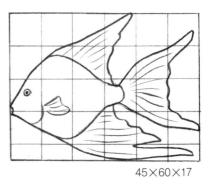

45×60×17

90×55×17

View of the positioning from above. It is important to be careful about placement, since good balance depends on it.

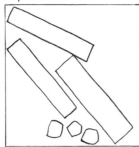

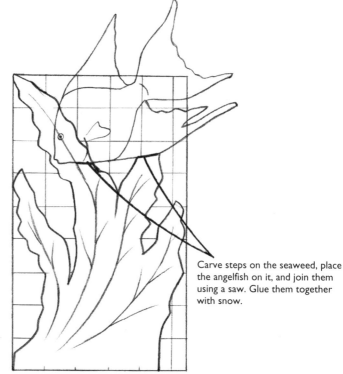

Carve steps on the seaweed, place the angelfish on it, and join them using a saw. Glue them together with snow.

90×55×25

The combination of an angelfish and seaweed. Make plenty of seaweed, and carve it so it seems to sway as if underwater. This effect can be created using a gouge chisel. Carve the lozenge-shaped body of an angelfish and sculpt big dorsal, ventral, and tail fins. It is important to make clear definitions of the border between each fin and the body. The method of making lines on the fins is the same as that for carving goldfish (see page 144).

142

ENDEAVOR

Color photograph on page 32.

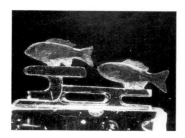

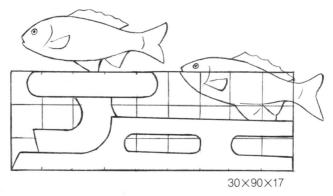

30×90×17

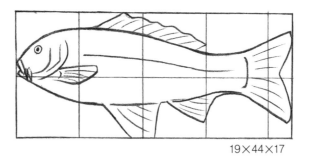

19×44×17

Carve two pairs of barbels (the whiskers) at the upper jaw.

Don't make the dorsal fin sharp. Carve the thick part with a flat chisel to make it look as if it is waving.

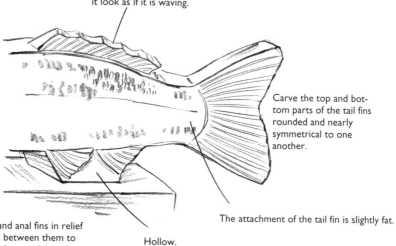

Carve the top and bottom parts of the tail fins rounded and nearly symmetrical to one another.

143

The attachment of the tail fin is slightly fat.

Hollow.

Carve the ventral and anal fins in relief so that ice remains between them to glue the figures on the stand. Join the fish to the stand using a saw, and glue the pieces with snow.

Characteristic features of carp are roundish bodies, two pairs of barbels on the upper lip, and spineless dorsal fins.

NOBLE SEAHORSE

Color photograph on page 33.

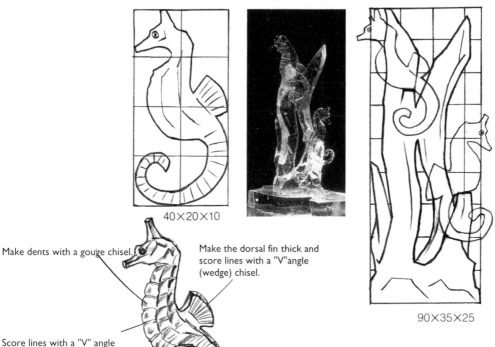

40×20×10

90×35×25

Make dents with a gouge chisel.

Make the dorsal fin thick and score lines with a "V"angle (wedge) chisel.

Score lines with a "V" angle (wedge) chisel.

Taper the tail by shaving the thin part thoroughly with a scroll saw and a pointed knife.

The characteristic feature of a seahorse is its vertical swimming figure with the tail curled inside; stand the body erect. The surface of the body is scaled like a reptile's. Carve the surface with a gouge chisel and an "V" angle chisel, and carve the whole body to make it look bony. Place the protruding stomach on the seaweed, join the pieces together using a saw, and glue them with snow.

FLOATING AMBER

Color photograph on page 34.

144

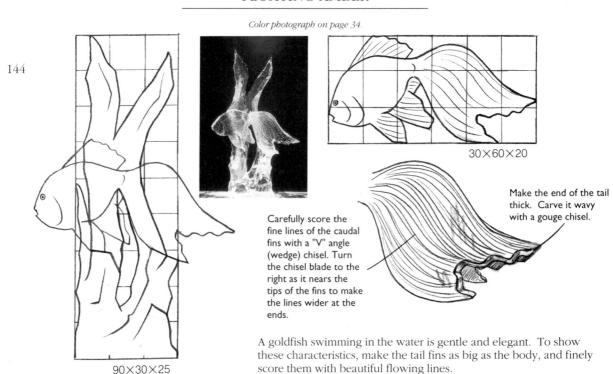

30×60×20

90×30×25

Carefully score the fine lines of the caudal fins with a "V" angle (wedge) chisel. Turn the chisel blade to the right as it nears the tips of the fins to make the lines wider at the ends.

Make the end of the tail thick. Carve it wavy with a gouge chisel.

A goldfish swimming in the water is gentle and elegant. To show these characteristics, make the tail fins as big as the body, and finely score them with beautiful flowing lines.

JUMP FOR JOY

Color photograph on page 36.

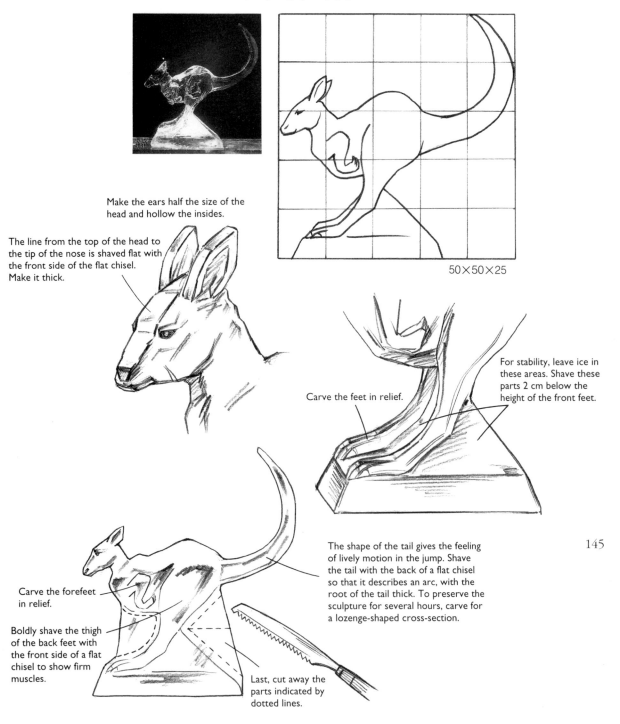

Make the ears half the size of the head and hollow the insides.

The line from the top of the head to the tip of the nose is shaved flat with the front side of the flat chisel. Make it thick.

$50 \times 50 \times 25$

Carve the feet in relief.

For stability, leave ice in these areas. Shave these parts 2 cm below the height of the front feet.

Carve the forefeet in relief.

Boldly shave the thigh of the back feet with the front side of a flat chisel to show firm muscles.

The shape of the tail gives the feeling of lively motion in the jump. Shave the tail with the back of a flat chisel so that it describes an arc, with the root of the tail thick. To preserve the sculpture for several hours, carve for a lozenge-shaped cross-section.

Last, cut away the parts indicated by dotted lines.

This is the instant a kangaroo is about to jump with its back feet—certainly a characteristic pose. Kangaroos have short, thin forefeet, and their hind legs are remarkably long and stout with developed muscles. Their tails are also thick and long. Pay attention to these features when drawing the pattern.

ANGEL'S CHAIR

Color photograph on page 37.

The fur grows thick, long, and soft. Carve the line of fur with a gouge chisel along the shape of the body. Show the change of the fur by the depth of the lines; in particular, deeply carve the area from the back up to the tail.

Carve the ears round.

Carve the cheeks with bulges.

Shave a little bit to show the lines of the forefeet.

Carve a hole with a flat chisel to make the space between the tail and tree and finish it with a scroll saw. Carve the grain of the wood with a gouge chisel.

$50 \times 55 \times 25$

Raccoons, which are very good at climbing trees, look much like raccoon dogs and have plump shapes. Show the figure eating nuts, slightly bending forward.

MY WAY

Color photograph on page 40.

146

Shave the back roughly with a gouge chisel to make it uneven, and with a scroll saw broadly score lines to show the fur standing on end. Carve roughly from the chest to the stomach with a gouge chisel, and make the unevenness clear. To show wildness, concentrate on carving the upper body with chisels.

Leave the ice between the two forefeet for support. To give more detail to the base, carve grass at the figure's feet.

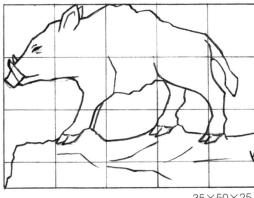

$35 \times 50 \times 25$

Place sharp tusks on the lower jaw.

It is important to show wildness when carving a boar. To do so, carve sharp tusks and fur lines on the upper body; sculpt the fur on the back standing on end.

TRAVELLER IN THE SNOW

Color photograph on page 38.

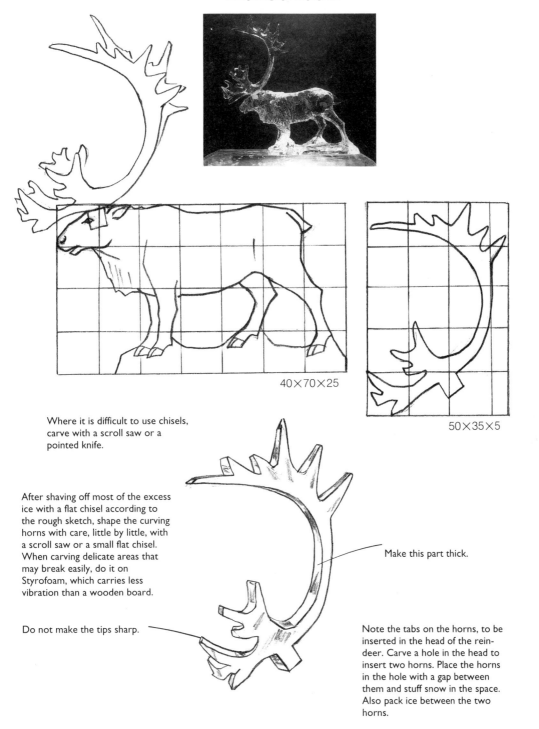

$40\times70\times25$

$50\times35\times5$

Where it is difficult to use chisels, carve with a scroll saw or a pointed knife.

After shaving off most of the excess ice with a flat chisel according to the rough sketch, shape the curving horns with care, little by little, with a scroll saw or a small flat chisel. When carving delicate areas that may break easily, do it on Styrofoam, which carries less vibration than a wooden board.

Make this part thick.

Do not make the tips sharp.

Note the tabs on the horns, to be inserted in the head of the reindeer. Carve a hole in the head to insert two horns. Place the horns in the hole with a gap between them and stuff snow in the space. Also pack ice between the two horns.

For a reindeer, accentuate the big, sharp, curved horns, the rough chest fur, the bony hooves, and the sturdy body. Use a large gouge chisel to carve large, rough lines of fur on the chest, a medium gouge chisel for smaller-scale fur lines, and a flat chisel for the back and the hind legs. To show wildness, it is better to carve concentrated lines of fur in one area rather than to carve fur lines all over the body.

OVER THE HORIZON

Color photograph on page 42.

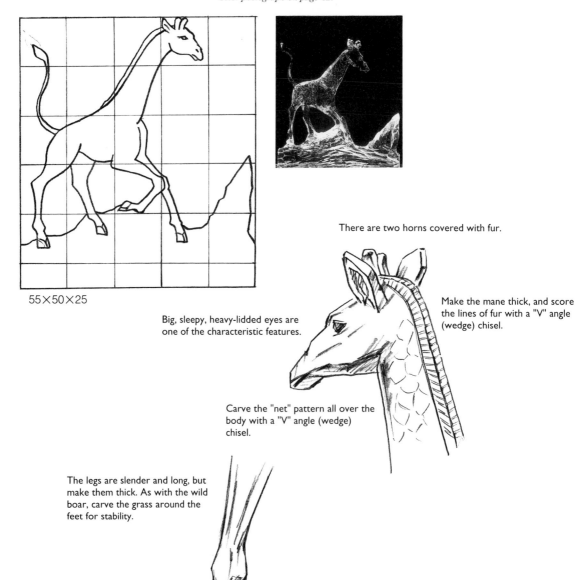

55×50×25

There are two horns covered with fur.

Make the mane thick, and score the lines of fur with a "V" angle (wedge) chisel.

Big, sleepy, heavy-lidded eyes are one of the characteristic features.

Carve the "net" pattern all over the body with a "V" angle (wedge) chisel.

The legs are slender and long, but make them thick. As with the wild boar, carve the grass around the feet for stability.

Shave the ankle by firmly placing a gouge chisel against the ice and slowly circling the chisel around once.

With a "V" angle (wedge) chisel, clearly carve the split hoof with a sharp tip.

148

Sculpt a giraffe with remarkably long legs and neck, and with slim lines overall. Also, carve the face widest at the top and narrower toward the mouth.

RELIEF ABC

Color photographs on pages 42 and 43.

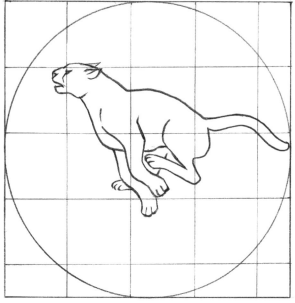

This design is a puma. The horizontal lines are carved from the reverse side with the tip of a gouge chisel. This method is effective for making the relief clear under back-lighting.

45×45×17

The characteristic features of the cocker spaniel are gentle eyes and a tufty coat. Clearly score the eyes with a "V" angle (wedge) chisel and scoop out around the eyes with a pointed knife. Use an electric drill with a round-edged bit (see page 185) to carve the line of fur, in order to show its lightness and softness. Carve the background with the front of a flat chisel, leaving blade marks to make it uneven.

149

45×55×17

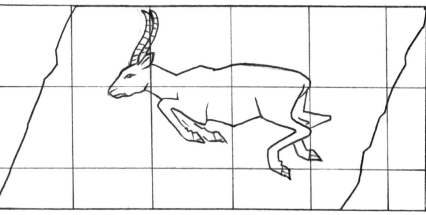

Carve the whole body of the gazelle with square lines, using a flat chisel. Abstractly carve the surrounding area with a flat chisel.

25×55×17

CINDERELLA

Color photograph on page 44.

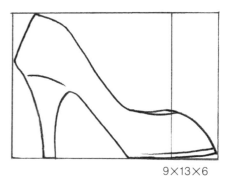

Carve a hollow in the shoe with a gouge chisel.

9×13×6

Carve the toe with a bulge to it, using the front of a flat chisel to shave it round little by little, as if shaving a round tree.

Carve a square heel with a flat chisel.

An ice high-heeled shoe made to look like a glass vase. It is good to add baby's breath as an accent.

BEAUTY

Color photograph on page 47.

Carve a hollow in the vase (indicated by dotted line), put in a sponge; then arrange the flowers.

150

To show softness in the locks of hair and the waistline, carve them with an electric drill with a round bit.

Using a gouge chisel, carve the clothes as if they are floating along the form of the body. The figure's grace can be further emphasized by making the hem fan out behind her.

A vase made in the shape of an elegant woman. To make her beautiful, have the figure bend slightly backward, and put her right leg ahead and her left leg behind. Choose small, pale flowers for the vase, and accent the blooms with green leaves.

100×55×25

HEARTSTRINGS

Color photograph on page 45.

C

18×14×3

D

D

26×9×3

B

23×23×3

Make these different heights.

Carve the contour with a pointed knife.

Scoop out the chin rest a little.

33×13×10

Carve the violin roughly according to the sketch, and finish it with a flat chisel.

A

10×10×10

Carve the chair accurately according to the size of each part. Join the parts using a saw, and glue them together with snow. Assemble them in the order of A, B, C, and D by joining them using a saw.

D is set into B.

D

C

B

A

151

A display for a small banquet: The combination of a violin and an antique chair, with a smilax (or vine) and a yellow rose for accents.

Color photograph on page 46.

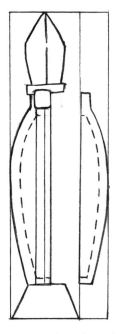

55×25×13

Side view: Carve the outline with the back of a flat chisel to make a soft bulge according to the rough sketches. Shave out the inside up to the dotted line. It is important to keep the wall thickness even. To do this, put your hands inside and outside to check the thickness during carving. If there is roughness inside, it will be impossible to achieve a beautiful line, because of the reflection of light. It is important to carve the walls carefully to make them smooth.

Put the flowers inside. After joining the vase halves with a saw, dribble a few drops of water on the seam and put the vase in the freezer to glue it.

Shave the out ice and put in flowers.

With a flat chisel, carve smooth the surfaces to be glued together.

A perfume bottle with baby's breath and eucalyptus leaves sealed inside. For an elegant atmosphere, use flowers and green lighting.

Color photographs on pages 48 and 49.

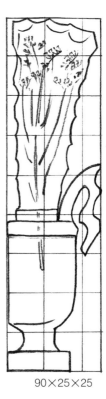

When the flower is inside most of the ice, it is better to roughly carve the ice with a flat chisel without detailed work. Carving it irregularly and on a large scale makes the roses look vivid.

When the flowers gather at the top of the ice, it is better to make the work represent-ational of something. To enhance the flowers, carve the ice around them sharply and deeply with a gouge chisel.

90×25×25

90×25×25

With a gouge chisel, carve a hole for the handle, and thoroughly finish it with a pointed knife.

Make only one surface flat; carve the rest round. To see how to achieve smooth contours, refer to page 194 for the description of carving columns.

Shave here by turning with a gouge chisel. Do this in the same way used to shave the foot of the wine glass (see page 157).

153

Sculptures of flowers frozen inside ice are generally called *ice flowers*. A key strategy for ice flowers is to design the works to complement the blooms. Also, it is important to use fresh flowers.

ROYAL CARRIAGE

Color photograph on page 50.

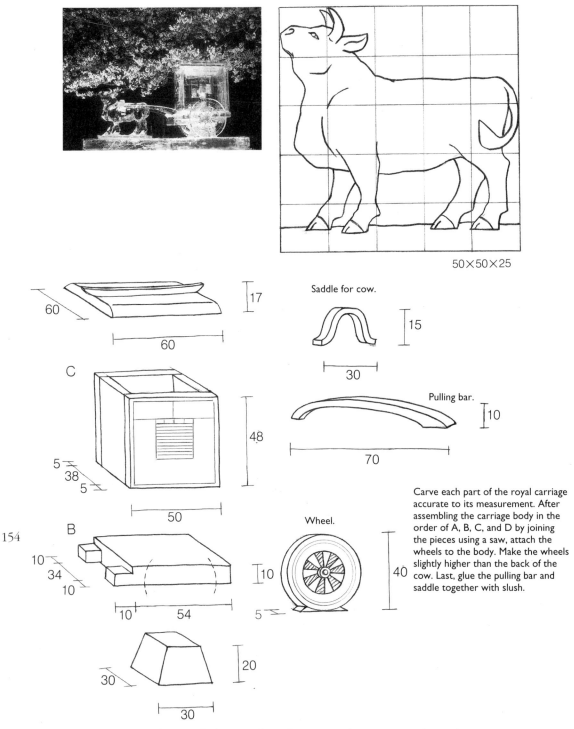

$50 \times 50 \times 25$

Saddle for cow.

15

30

C

48

5
38
5

50

Pulling bar.

10

70

60

17

60

Wheel.

10

5

40

Carve each part of the royal carriage accurate to its measurement. After assembling the carriage body in the order of A, B, C, and D by joining the pieces using a saw, attach the wheels to the body. Make the wheels slightly higher than the back of the cow. Last, glue the pulling bar and saddle together with slush.

154

B

10
34
10

10   54

30

30

20

Carve the cow thick-set, and emphasize its volume. It is good to make the height of the cow half that of the carriage. To show movement, turn the face upward. After roughly shaping the cow with a saw according to the sketch, carve it with a flat chisel from the top toward the bottom; in particular, carve roughly from the back to the buttocks, and make it look bony.

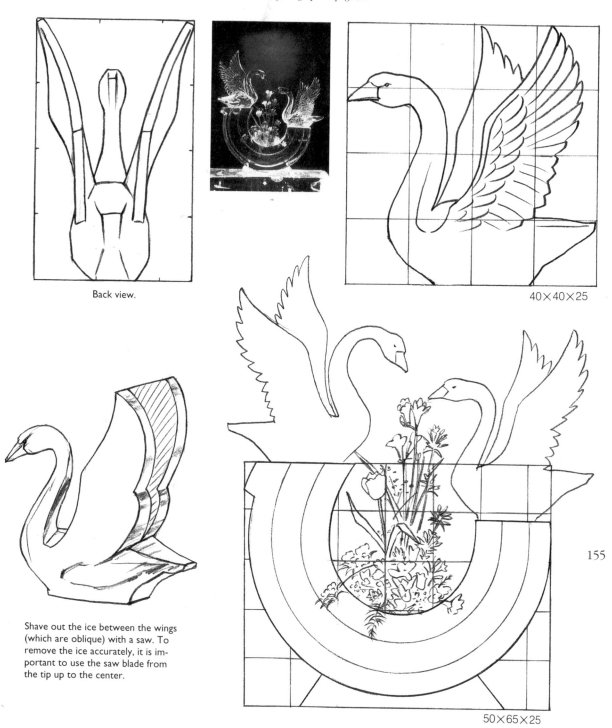

Back view.

40×40×25

Shave out the ice between the wings (which are oblique) with a saw. To remove the ice accurately, it is important to use the saw blade from the tip up to the center.

50×65×25

155

This is a composition of swans watching flowers. To utilize the flowers effectively, the choices of kind, size, and color are important. It is good to combine two swans with their wings open wide for displays at celebratory occasions such as weddings. Refer to page 127 for how to carve swans.

Color photograph on page 53.

50×22×22

22×22×22

Refer to page 190 for how to carve a ball.

View from above.

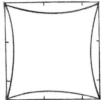

Carve with the back of a flat chisel to make symmetrical curves.

Draw accurate measurements on all four surfaces of the posts, and according to the measurements, shave them to a taper with the front of a flat chisel.

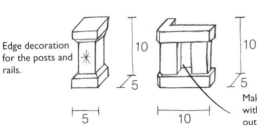

70×24×24

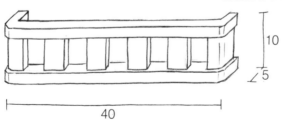

Edge decoration for the posts and rails.

10

5

5

10

10

5

5

10

Make the space by carving a hole with a flat chisel and cutting the rest out with a scroll saw. Finish it using a flat chisel for vertical and horizontal lines, and make the surfaces smooth.

10

5

40

156

This is a composition of a ball and posts. The compositional balance is key for this kind of simple sculpture. The surface of the ice has a beautiful luster, effected by the lighting arrangement: Blue lights are placed inside a table specially designed for displaying ice, and blue light is shined on the sculpture diagonally from the right front.

SIMPLICITY

Color photograph on page 54.

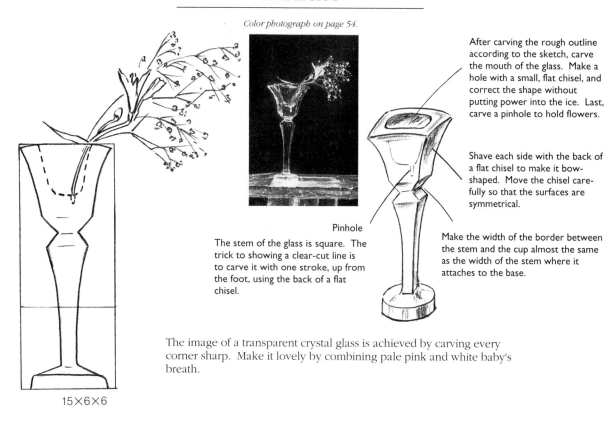

After carving the rough outline according to the sketch, carve the mouth of the glass. Make a hole with a small, flat chisel, and correct the shape without putting power into the ice. Last, carve a pinhole to hold flowers.

Shave each side with the back of a flat chisel to make it bow-shaped. Move the chisel carefully so that the surfaces are symmetrical.

Pinhole

The stem of the glass is square. The trick to showing a clear-cut line is to carve it with one stroke, up from the foot, using the back of a flat chisel.

Make the width of the border between the stem and the cup almost the same as the width of the stem where it attaches to the base.

15×6×6

The image of a transparent crystal glass is achieved by carving every corner sharp. Make it lovely by combining pale pink and white baby's breath.

GLASS WITHIN A GLASS

Color photograph on page 55.

When the shape of the body is almost finished, stand the ice and shave the foot of the glass. Move the blade of a gouge chisel forward little by little and go around the block.

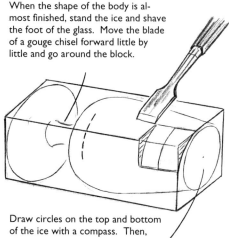

157

Draw circles on the top and bottom of the ice with a compass. Then, after drawing accurate sketches on the four surfaces, lay the ice on its side. Shave the excess ice away in the same way as when carving poles (refer to page 194), using the front of a flat chisel.

37×18×18

An entertaining and enjoyable effect can be achieved by carving a wine glass using ice made with a wine glass frozen inside it. It is good to spread crushed ice around the base when displaying this work. The most important step in producing this work is to accurately draw the sketches on the four surfaces of the ice.

PREDATOR

Color photograph on page 56.

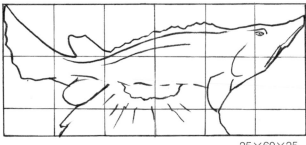

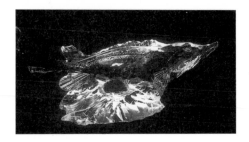

$25 \times 60 \times 25$

View from above: Be careful with the way the sturgeon curves.

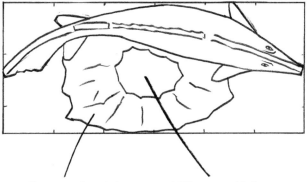

Front view: Place a glass dish inside the dotted line. Carve diagonally to make flowing water.

Carve a rough conical shape with a gouge chisel.

With a gouge chisel, make a hollow in which to place a glass dish.

Shave while making gradations with the back of a flat chisel.

158

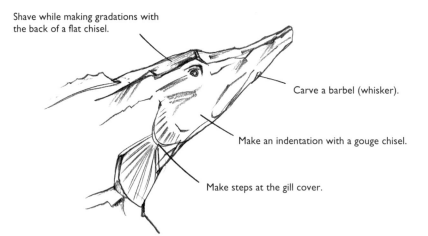

Carve a barbel (whisker).

Make an indentation with a gouge chisel.

Make steps at the gill cover.

This is a sturgeon with a dish to serve caviar. Carve the entire sturgeon ruggedly. To do so, carve the thickness of the area between the mouth and the dorsal fin with steps, using the back of a flat chisel, and roughly score the surface of the body and the dorsal fin with a "V" angle (wedge) chisel to make the unevenness apparent.

SPLASH

Color photograph on page 57.

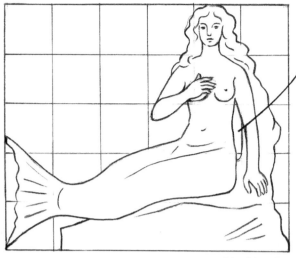

Carve out a space, to emphasize the waist.

Give the shell thickness, and with a gouge chisel, score the outside with wide lines as an accent. Also make a hole at the bottom so that water can drain.

50×60×25

A mermaid and a shell. Put a glass dish in the shell and serve caviar in it. This is an example of buffet service. Place napkins on a tray and cover with blue cellophane, then spread crushed ice over them for a beautiful blue color that appears and disappears in the surface of ice, which conveys a refreshing feeling.

Carve the mermaid using the following procedure. First, chip the upper body roughly with a gouge chisel as if scooping it, and make the lower body plump. Be sure to make the area around the attachment of the tail fin thick, and carve scales deep along the body with a gouge chisel. Carve the facial features clearly; carve the hair roughly with a gouge chisel.

IGLOO

Color photograph on page 58.

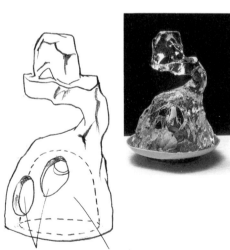

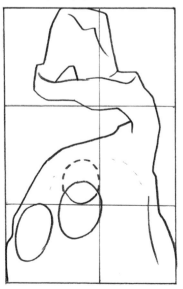

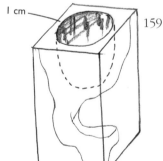

1 cm

159

Make these holes when finishing the work.

Inside of the dotted line is a cave.

Draw a rough sketch on the ice and position it upside down. Make a hole with a gouge chisel, leaving 1 cm to the edge. Then turn the ice right side up and carve the entire thing.

28×18×18

Display for sashimi. Carve it in the image of an igloo.

PROUD PEACOCK

Color photograph on page 59.

25×40×25

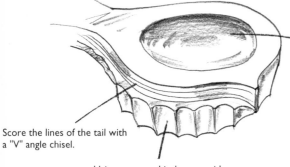

Make a shallow cup. It is good to line the hollow with a big leaf or a bamboo screen to prevent food from slipping.

Score the lines of the tail with a "V" angle chisel.

Using a gouge chisel, carve wide scoops from top to bottom to accent.

Carve the tail of the peacock to make it a bowl for Chinese appetizers. Make the dish slant slightly to drain the water.

SWEETNESS

Color photograph on page 64.

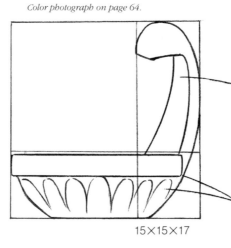

Shave it so that the cross section becomes diamond shaped, similar to the carved swan's neck.

Score a line with a "V" angle chisel. Shave the area under the line as if peeling away a skin, and decorate it by moving a gouge chisel with broad strokes from top to bottom to make the pattern.

15×15×17

A fruit dish as a focal point for small banquets. It is suitable for serving small fruits such as cherries. Make a pinhole so that water drains.

LOBSTER

Color photograph on page 60.

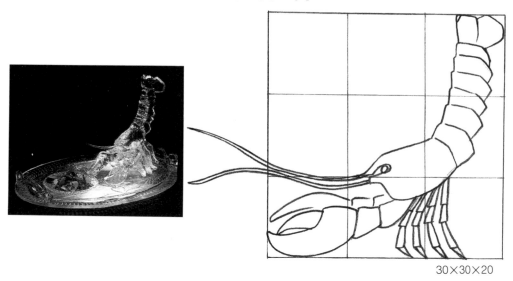

$30 \times 30 \times 20$

View of the tray from above.

$40 \times 70 \times 10$

Carve the pattern from the under-side with a gouge chisel.

161

Profile of the tray.

A lobster and a tray suitable for a cold lobster dish. Carving the lobster and attaching it effectively enhances the cuisine. Carve two claws, one the mirror-image of, but bigger than, the other. It is important to make sketches while carefully observing a real lobster. Carve the antennae separately. Carve them slightly thicker than they need to be and adjust the size by soaking them in flowing water. Then glue them to the body, putting snow at the joint in a freezing room.

THE WINNER

Color photograph on page 62.

Holding a chisel in one hand, carefully shave the outside while placing the other hand inside to gauge the thickness of the ice.

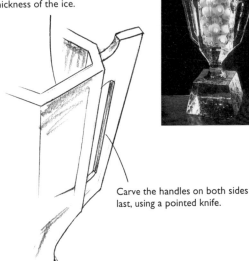

First draw accurate sketches on the top and sides. Carve out the interior of the cup from the top, then carve the outline of it on the sides with a flat chisel.

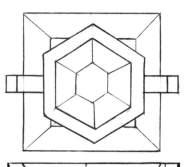

Carve the handles on both sides last, using a pointed knife.

Victory cup suitable for celebrations such as the end of a golf tournament. This is good for cold dessert and is also suitable for champagne. It is important to achieve uniform thickness in the cup.

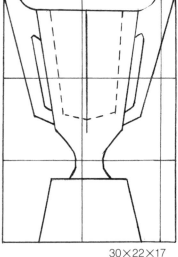

30×22×17

DELICIOUS

Color photograph on page 63.

162

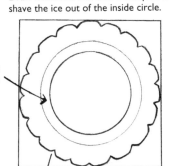

The decoration around the opening: Draw double circles with a compass and shave the ice out of the inside circle.

The surface that attaches to the body.

18×18×3

Carve this in the shape of a horn. Shave the curve with the back of a flat chisel.

Carve in the shape of a V with a "V" angle chisel and shave away the corners to make them round.

30×20×17

Lay the decoration for the opening flat and place the body on it. Glue the pieces together with several drops of water.

An abstract dish for ice cream. Carve the decoration that rings the opening separately and glue it to the body.

BASKET OF FRUIT

Color photograph on page 66.

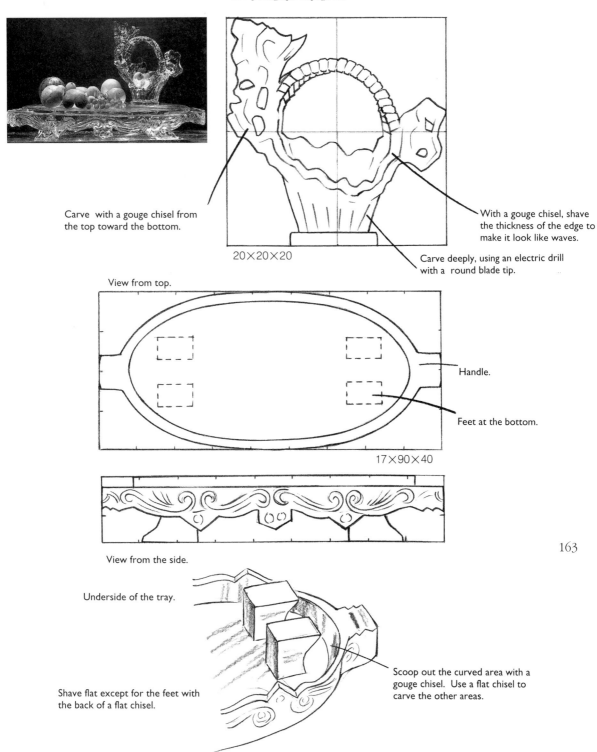

Carve with a gouge chisel from the top toward the bottom.

With a gouge chisel, shave the thickness of the edge to make it look like waves.

20×20×20

Carve deeply, using an electric drill with a round blade tip.

View from top.

Handle.

Feet at the bottom.

17×90×40

View from the side.

Underside of the tray.

Scoop out the curved area with a gouge chisel. Use a flat chisel to carve the other areas.

Shave flat except for the feet with the back of a flat chisel.

163

A basket and a tray suitable for serving fruit. A decoration that looks like a vine of grapes (carved with an electric drill with a round blade bit) accents the basket. Carve the decorative patterns on the side of the tray with the same drill, gouging it 1 cm deep.

MELODY OF LOVE

Color photograph on page 67.

Draw a sketch of the clef on the ice and carve according to the guide lines.

G

The order of setting (do it in a freezer room): Attach 12 of equally spaced E to platform A by joining them using a saw. Join the vertical sides of the 12 Es together at the center. Sprinkle several drops of water and glue them together. Continue gluing as you place platform B, three 25 cm long Fs, platform C, three 20 cm long Fs, and platform D, in that order, and finally the clef, at the top.

Shave flat the area that will be joined using a saw. Make the clef thicker at the bottom, tapering toward the top.

25

D

A hexagon with a diameter of 25 cm.

10

30

2

20

2

25

2

20

5

F

3

Prepare six columns, three 25 cm long and three 20 cm long.

C

30

A hexagon with a diameter of 30 cm.

B

30

A hexagon with a diameter of 30 cm.

E

Shave the curved area with the back of a flat chisel.

2

20

20

Prepare 12 of these, carved according to the measurements.

A stand for petits fours. Carve each part accurately according to the measurements and join them together using a saw. Calculate suitable size and thickness according to the duration of the occasion.

A

45

A dodecagon with a diameter of 45 cm.

DRIVE AROUND THE BLUE LAGOON

Color photograph on page 65.

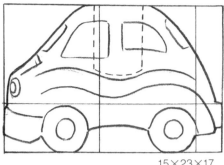

15×23×17

View from the front.

An antique car carved for serving tropical drinks. Create an antique image by giving roundness to the entire body. Make a hollow (dotted-line area) with a gouge chisel from the top and carve out the space for a drink. It is important to be very careful about the thickness of the sides.

A. PONCET, *FUGUE EXPAND*

Color photograph on page 68.

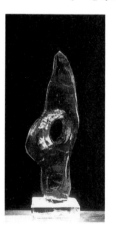

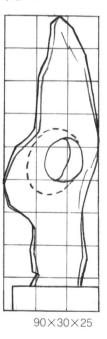

90×30×25

The image suggests a petrified tree, dug out and stood on its roots. The balance between the space and the bulge is important, and it is good to make the bulge slightly lower than half the height of the sculpture. Carve the space with an electric saw first, in the shape of a cross, and then around the cross make a round hollow with a gouge chisel. Use a flat chisel for carving the rest.

T. KASAI, *KENCHO*

Color photograph on page 68.

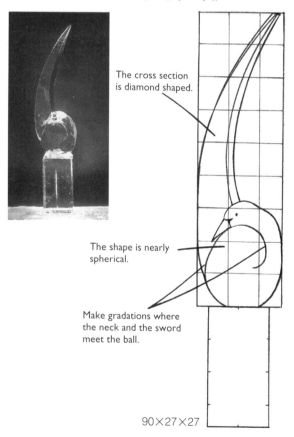

The cross section is diamond shaped.

The shape is nearly spherical.

Make gradations where the neck and the sword meet the ball.

90×27×27

An abstract combination of a ball and a sword, carved the way a bird sleeps, rolling up its body. To keep balance, it is better to use a rectangular stand for works flowing vertically.

HOWLING WIND

Color photograph on page 69.

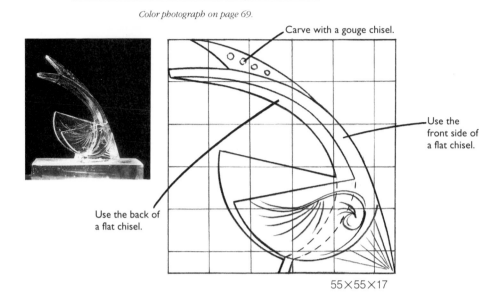

Carve with a gouge chisel.

Use the front side of a flat chisel.

Use the back of a flat chisel.

55×55×17

Shave between the feathers with a scroll saw and a flat chisel to make a space. One key to success is to saw from the center to the tip of the blade. To show movement, make the wings semicircular, and place them with one pointed up and the other down. Carve the neckline using the front and the back of the flat chisel.

TRIANGLE OF HOPE

Color photograph on page 70.

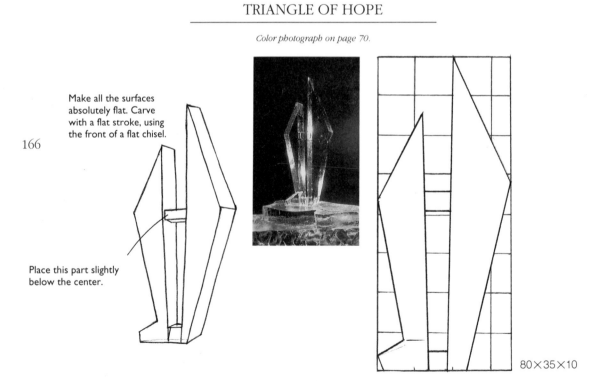

Make all the surfaces absolutely flat. Carve with a flat stroke, using the front of a flat chisel.

Place this part slightly below the center.

80×35×10

166

The visual balance between the two triangles rises upward and leads to a horizontal line as the focal point. For banquets, it is good to use larger measurements and place flowers on the horizontal bar.

BIRDS OF THE SOUTH WIND

Color photograph on page 71.

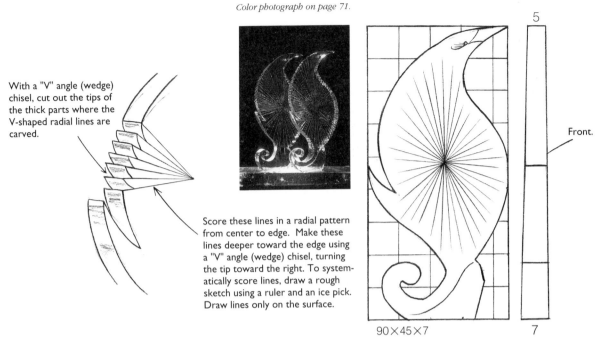

With a "V" angle (wedge) chisel, cut out the tips of the thick parts where the V-shaped radial lines are carved.

Score these lines in a radial pattern from center to edge. Make these lines deeper toward the edge using a "V" angle (wedge) chisel, turning the tip toward the right. To systematically score lines, draw a rough sketch using a ruler and an ice pick. Draw lines only on the surface.

5

Front.

90×45×7

7

Side view: Be careful with the thickness of the top and bottom parts.

Carved abstractly, this recalls a bird that inhabits the tropics. When light hits the carved radial lines, they look like stretched threads, which breathes life into the work.

G. SUGIMOTO, *THE EARTH*

Color photograph on page 72.

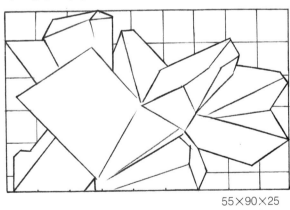

167

55×90×25

A carved image of the instant when ice is dropped on the earth, the sculpture is made by cutting it boldly, using a large flat chisel. With different lighting, the work can look like iron or a rock of crystal. Think out your choice of color depending on the image.

K. AKAOGI, *STRIPE ARCH*

Color photograph on page 74.

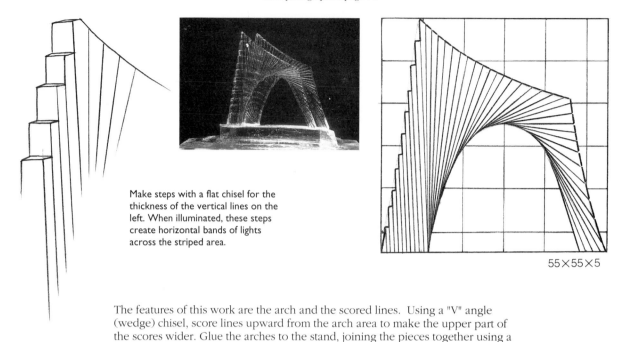

Make steps with a flat chisel for the thickness of the vertical lines on the left. When illuminated, these steps create horizontal bands of lights across the striped area.

55×55×5

The features of this work are the arch and the scored lines. Using a "V" angle (wedge) chisel, score lines upward from the arch area to make the upper part of the scores wider. Glue the arches to the stand, joining the pieces together using a saw.

SWAN TRIO

Color photograph on page 77.

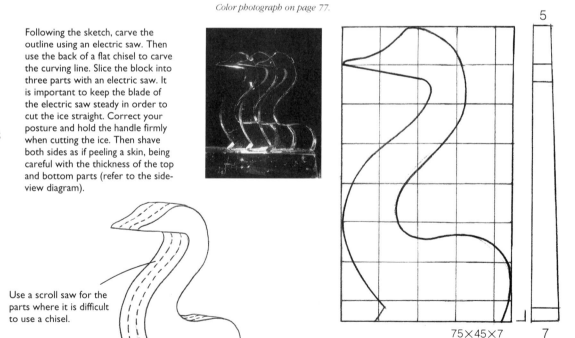

Following the sketch, carve the outline using an electric saw. Then use the back of a flat chisel to carve the curving line. Slice the block into three parts with an electric saw. It is important to keep the blade of the electric saw steady in order to cut the ice straight. Correct your posture and hold the handle firmly when cutting the ice. Then shave both sides as if peeling a skin, being careful with the thickness of the top and bottom parts (refer to the side-view diagram).

168

Use a scroll saw for the parts where it is difficult to use a chisel.

5

75×45×7

7

Side view.

This is a simple work composed of curves and planes carved in the image of a swan. By lining up three swans, this work captures the motif of swans flying in formation.

FLOWERY FLAKES OF SNOW

Color photograph on page 76.

15×15×1.5

Snow crystals. The appropriate size of this work when used for banquets is 50 centimeters high and 10 centimeters thick. With a compass, draw a circle on a perfect square, then draw lines to divide the circle accurately into six. Along these lines, draw a symmetrical sketch. Carve with a scroll saw and a flat chisel, and use a pointed knife for curves.

O. ZADKINE SCULPTURE

Color photograph on page 79.

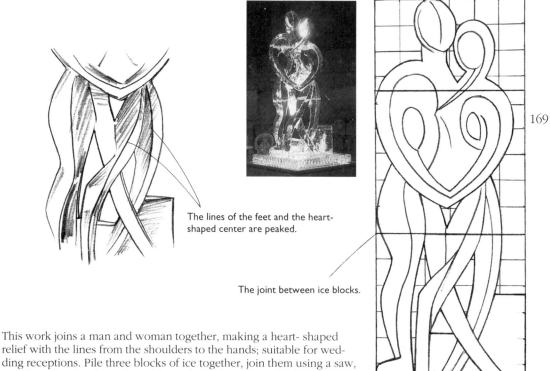

The lines of the feet and the heart-shaped center are peaked.

The joint between ice blocks.

169

This work joins a man and woman together, making a heart- shaped relief with the lines from the shoulders to the hands; suitable for wedding receptions. Pile three blocks of ice together, join them using a saw, and draw the sketch on them. Carve the outline along the sketch marks, using a flat chisel. The back of the work is flat.

145×60×25

A. ARCHIPENKO, *STANDING NUDE II*

Color photograph on page 78.

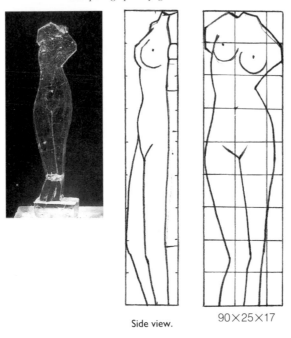

Side view.   90×25×17

The silhouette is the focus. The basic consideration for the composition of the human body is to place the pubis at the center. Carve the torso and flowing waist flat.

RECLINING NUDE

Color photograph on page 78.

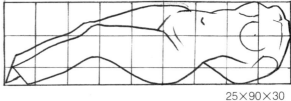

25×90×30

Stand the ice up and draw the sketch on it. Carve roughly with a flat chisel. Then lay the ice down to finish carving it, leaving traces of the chisel blade.

Torso. Carve the depression of the waist and the rise of the breast, and make the body line clear to give a three dimensional impression.

PEACOCK'S SPRING LIGHT

Color photograph on page 80.

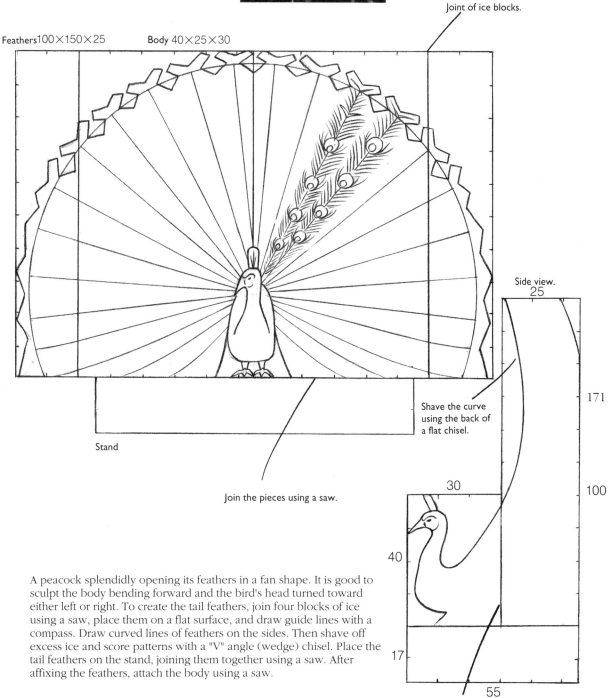

Joint of ice blocks.

Feathers 100×150×25   Body 40×25×30

Side view.
25

171

100

Shave the curve
using the back of
a flat chisel.

Stand

Join the pieces using a saw.

30

40

17

55

Join the parts using a saw.

A peacock splendidly opening its feathers in a fan shape. It is good to sculpt the body bending forward and the bird's head turned toward either left or right. To create the tail feathers, join four blocks of ice using a saw, place them on a flat surface, and draw guide lines with a compass. Draw curved lines of feathers on the sides. Then shave off excess ice and score patterns with a "V" angle (wedge) chisel. Place the tail feathers on the stand, joining them together using a saw. After affixing the feathers, attach the body using a saw.

SEAHORSES IN THE SPRING WATER OF APOLLON

Color photograph on pages 82 and 83.

Express the movements of the seahorses by giving character to each one, varying the height and the positions of their necks and their tail fins. Show the energy of vigorous swimming through the way the bodies twist and the size and profile of the tail fins. Show the action of moving forward by carving the forefeet vigorously stroking the water.

To show the energy, carve the tail fins with sweeping movements.

Neptune. Sculpt the figure bending forward, guiding the seahorses. Using a gouge chisel and a flat chisel, score the clothes to make them look as if they are blowing in the wind.

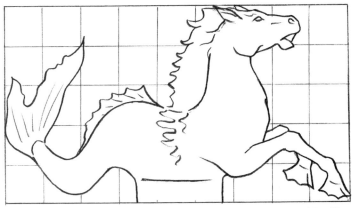

50×90×25

Use a gouge chisel. Score important parts using a "V" angle (wedge) chisel to show detail.

Webbed. Be careful that the shape is not that of a hoof.

172

65×70×25

Triton. Emphasize both the balance between the hands and the gesture and expression of the figure calling seahorses with a shell horn.

50×45×25

Create a fantastic atmosphere by combining three seahorses. Float the sculpture on water and light it with yellow to make it look mythical.

AURORA

Color photograph on page 84.

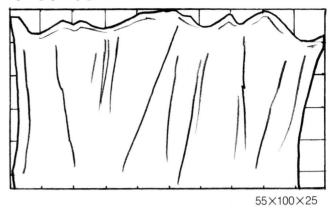

Using the back of a flat chisel, shave the work in long strokes, as if scooping, and give it thickness.

55×100×25

Carve both the front and the back with a gouge chisel to make the work wavy.

This is an image of the aurora borealis, the beautiful natural light that appears in arctic regions. Capture the aurora's atmosphere by carving waving stripe patterns all over the ice with a gouge chisel.

POSEIDON'S DREAM MISSION

Color photograph on page 88.

Score lines using a "V" angle (wedge) chisel. Use an electric drill with a round-tipped bit.

Make the boy with the body of Cupid.   50×80×25

173

Carve a dolphin roughly, leaving traces of tool marks by properly using the front and the back of a flat chisel.

View from top.

This is a scene of a boy riding on a dolphin. This amusing work is appropriate for many kinds of banquets.

A FLOCK OF REINDEER

Color photograph on page 94.

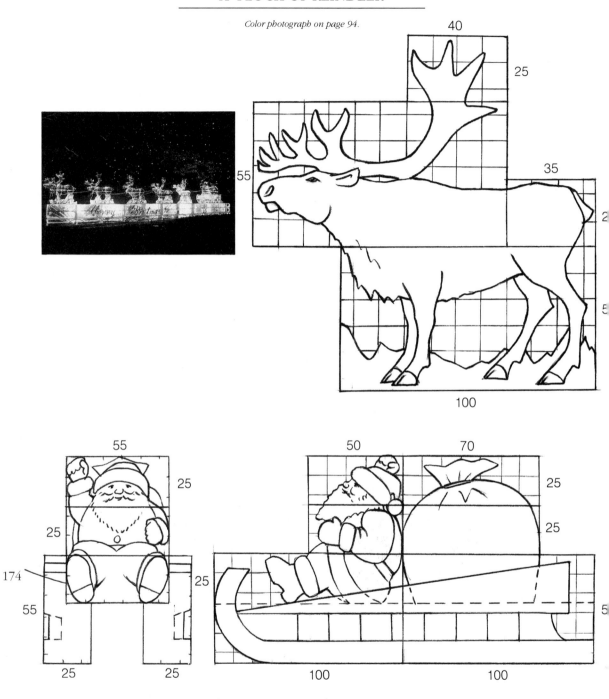

Created for a Christmastime event, this piece was carved for outdoor display. When setting the piece outside, consider the silhouette's appearance from different sides, and carve the outline roughly, giving thickness to the figures. Make Santa Claus's features well defined, and the lines of his suit, beard, and shoes clear. Refer to page 147 for how to carve reindeer.

SILVER HARP

Color photograph on page 96.

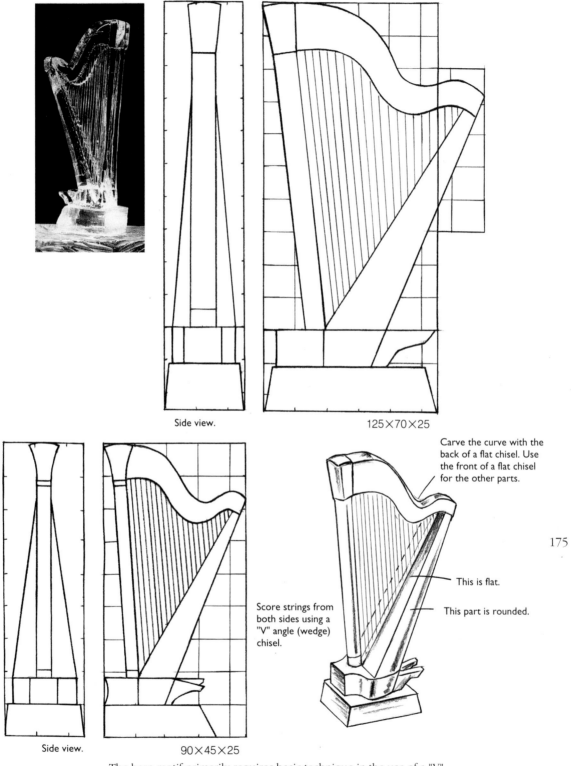

Side view.

125×70×25

Side view.

90×45×25

Carve the curve with the back of a flat chisel. Use the front of a flat chisel for the other parts.

This is flat.

This part is rounded.

Score strings from both sides using a "V" angle (wedge) chisel.

175

The harp motif primarily requires basic technique in the use of a "V" angle (wedge) chisel and the front and back of a flat chisel. When carving the assembled ice pieces, it is important that the joint not run horizontally through the harp strings.

TWILIGHT

Color photograph on page 97.

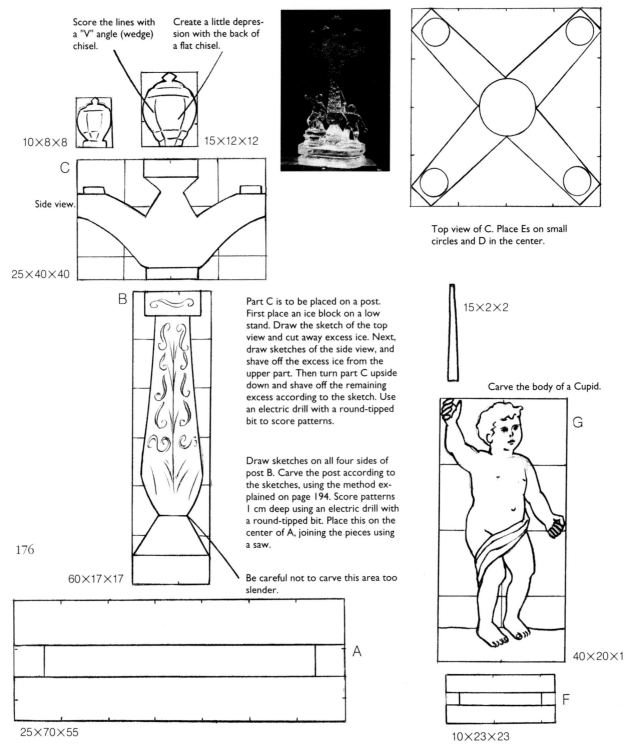

Score the lines with a "V" angle (wedge) chisel.

Create a little depression with the back of a flat chisel.

10×8×8

15×12×12

C

Side view.

25×40×40

Top view of C. Place Es on small circles and D in the center.

B

15×2×2

Carve the body of a Cupid.

G

Part C is to be placed on a post. First place an ice block on a low stand. Draw the sketch of the top view and cut away excess ice. Next, draw sketches of the side view, and shave off the excess ice from the upper part. Then turn part C upside down and shave off the remaining excess according to the sketch. Use an electric drill with a round-tipped bit to score patterns.

Draw sketches on all four sides of post B. Carve the post according to the sketches, using the method explained on page 194. Score patterns 1 cm deep using an electric drill with a round-tipped bit. Place this on the center of A, joining the pieces using a saw.

176

60×17×17

Be careful not to carve this area too slender.

40×20×1

A

F

25×70×55

10×23×23

A street lamp. Draw sketches accurately, according to the measurements. Stack the carved parts by joining them with a saw in the order A, B, C, D, E. Then place F and G on A, joining them using a saw.

Color photograph on page 176.

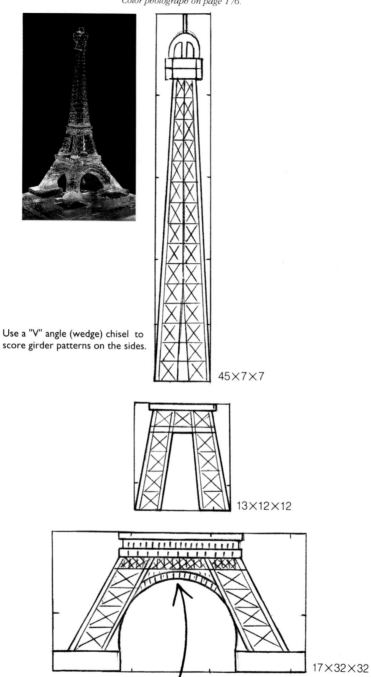

Use a "V" angle (wedge) chisel to
score girder patterns on the sides.

45×7×7

13×12×12

17×32×32

Shave the arches with a gouge chisel.

The Eiffel Tower is assembled by carving three parts and joining them
together using a saw. On the four sides of each part, draw the sketches
accurate to the measurements. Then carve the ice with a flat chisel,
following to the sketches.

CONCORDE

Color photograph on page 99.

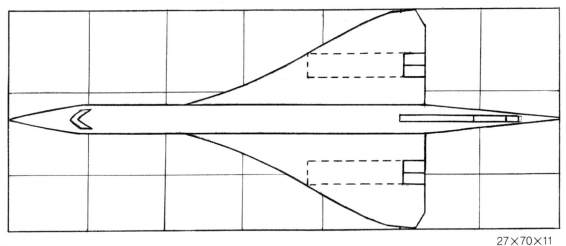

27×70×11

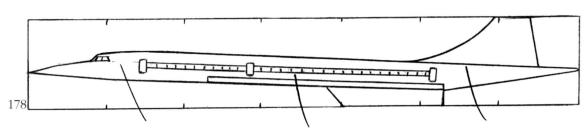

178

Shave the roundness of the body with the front of a flat chisel, in the same manner as carving a pole.

Score the windows using a "V" angle (wedge) chisel.

The tail is joined to the fuselage using a saw.

A miniature Concorde. Draw accurate sketches on the top and sides of the ice and shave off the excess. Carve the plane's tail separately, using a flat chisel. After joining it to the body using a saw, glue it with a few drops of water and let it set in a freezing room. Perform all the work on a Styrofoam board, because this is a very delicate piece.

BRONTOSAURUS

Color photograph on page 100.

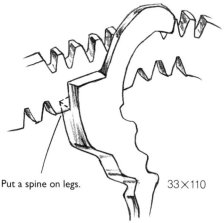

Put a spine on legs.   33×110

Enlarge the plans of a brontosaurus dinosaur model kit to make the width 110 centimeters, and carve it. The important consid-eration in applying this model to ice sculpture is to place the backbone on the feet *after* joining the four feet in their positions on the stand. Use a saw, firmly fix the feet with snow, and draw sketches so that the backbone can be placed on the feet. Assemble the parts in a freezer room and put a few drops of water on the joints to glue them together.

CONGRATULATIONS

Color photograph on page 102.

42×22×5   Front. 5   3

MERRY CHRISTMAS

Color photograph on page 102.

179

31×130×3

Side view: The front is straight and the back becomes thicker at the bottom.

It is convenient to make paper templates in advance and to use them when sketching the letters. Carve from top to bottom. Use a pointed knife or a scroll saw when carving the small parts.

Basics of Ice Sculpture

What Is Ice Sculpture?

Ice sculpture ranges from large-scale, artistic works produced from a block of ice (or several joined blocks), to small-scale, practical works such as a decorative support for a dish (which is also called ice handiwork). The use of ice sculpture is widespread: for decorations to heighten the atmosphere of banquets at hotels and restaurants, for serving-dishes, for television commercials, for department store promotions, and for many other kinds of events.

Ice sculpture used outdoors, such as for winter carnivals, is different from an indoor display. Outdoors, splendid large-scale works using natural ice can be created and displayed to entertain audiences. Ice sculpture festivals, such as those that take place every year in Hokkaido, Japan, have become a tradition that lends poetic charm to winter. Thus ice sculpture is not just for bringing coolness in the summertime, but is an integral part of all seasons.

The number of carvers of ice sculpture increases every year. It is thought that there are currently more than 10,000 carvers in Japan—including Western cuisine chefs working in hotels and restaurants as well as Japanese-cuisine chefs and bartenders.

Ice sculpture in Japan is said to have begun when the late Tokuzo Akiyama, head chef of the Imperial Household Agency during the Taisho era (1912–26), carved a trial work after a trip to France, where he had seen carved ice used as a dish for food. However, it was not until the 1930s, during the Showa era (1926–89), that ice sculpture became popular. The spread of ice sculpture owes much to the efforts of the late Shuko Kobayashi, the first chairman of the Japan Ice Sculpture Association, and to the establishment of an annual competition. The ice sculpture competition was first held in Tokyo, in 1955, sponsored by the ice manufacturing industry as a promotional measure when the demand for ice fell with the proliferation of refrigerators after World War II. Since then the competition has been held every year. It became a nationwide competition in 1972. Another great influence were the classes held around the country by the late sculptor Shuko Kobayashi, beginning in 1957 or 1958. It was Kobayashi who advanced the idea of making large-sized works for hotels, and it was around this time that large-scale ice works came to be called "ice sculpture." Also influential was the improvement of the flat chisel, which is easy to use.

In 1964, the Tokyo Olympics were held. Many hotels were built throughout Japan, with large guest rooms and banquet facilities. The adoption of the then-novel buffet style of entertaining led to a search for new devices for decoration and presentation. Ice sculpture attracted a great deal of attention as a center point for large banquets that produced a magnificent atmosphere.

With the subsequent "hotel rush," the demand for ice sculpture increased, and large scale works became predominant. I believe that ice sculpture spread and improved because of the demand of the times. With greater interest and more practi-tioners, ice-sculpture technique naturally became more advanced.

It goes without saying that a grounding in basic technique is important for ice sculpture, just as it is for cooking. Having established a sound base, new technique will evolve. It is important to have this attitude when tackling ice sculpture.

Basics of Decoration for Parties

Ice sculpture presents images. But image is not everything: there must be a theme. The theme must be suitable both for the purpose of the work and for the environment where the work will be placed–when, where, and at what kind of banquet the work is to be used–and it must be a theme that balances with the food.

Therein lies the difficulty and the joy of "subzero art" which disappears in time.

A swan that looks rough at first will show a neat silhouette in time, when the banquet reaches full swing. That unfolding beauty is the strong point of ice sculpture. Ice sculpture is created with the clear understanding that ice is to melt, and the sculptor calculates accordingly. There is absolutely no forgiveness for mistakes that result in crumbling ice sculptures halfway through a banquet.

When the subject to be carved is thin and has light parts, it would melt in an instant if carved as the actual subject looked. For example, the beak of a hawk has a thin, sharp tip. But if carved the way a real beak looks,the ice melts as time passes by and the beak becomes round, losing its characteristic shape. Accordingly, we carve using a method that makes the thickness of the beak inconspicuous, making it look thin in profile but thick if seen from the front.

Volume is important regardless of the size of the works. It is better to skillfully represent characteristic features by carving the whole body rough, to give a certain impression of heaviness, than to show delicateness and precision by giving fine lines to the ice.

To best enhance the works, you should use lighting and flower arrangements. Because ice bends light as glass does, it is good to spotlight ice with this refractive characteristic in mind. However, that doesn't mean it is enough to merely illuminate the works. There are ways of lighting that are most suitable for banquets, and it is necessary to think out ahead of time the method and color of lighting to be used. White or pale-hued spotlights, such as pale blue and pale purple, usually produce good coloring. Since many kinds of lighting are used, flowers of vivid primary colors can create an imbalance. Again, pale colors are more effective.

When sketching subjects, especially living creatures, it is important to grasp their unique characteristics and habits. To accomplish this, it is helpful to study them by observing living subjects as well as consulting illustrated books.

Ice and Its Temperature

Currently, there are not any specialized forms of ice for ice sculpture. We use ice manufactured at ice houses, and it comes in what are called "commercial blocks." These square-shaped, pillarlike commercial blocks are, in Japan, 100 centimeters high by 55 centimeters wide by 25 centimeters thick, and weigh 135 kilograms. In the United States the standard sizes are 40 inches by 20 inches by 10 inches (300 pounds) and 60 inches by 20 inches by 10 inches (425 pounds). These blocks are sold whole or cut to size, accord-ing to use.

The ice most suitable for sculpture is that which has little "snow" (opaque white areas) in the center of the block, which is caused by air bubble contamination during manufacturing. Good ice has high transparency and is hard. Of course, avoid ice that is cracked or has visible scars on its surface.

When creating sculpture, use ice kept for one day at temperature of $-4°C$ (25°F) after being manufactured. If ice is kept colder than $-4°C$, it becomes too hard and cracks when brought to a warmer place.

Ice sculpture is created most often in kitchens. When carving ice sculpture, choose a place where it is neither sunny nor breezy. Also, it is important to keep the finished works at around $-8°C$ (18°F).

THE VARIETY OF TOOLS AND THEIR USAGE

The following explains the tools needed to sculpt ice. It is important to use the proper tools for the size of the intended work.

● "V" Angle (Wedge) Chisel

A. "V" angle chisel (large) The length of the blade is 30 mm and the length of the handle is 380 mm. Used primarily for finishing large, multi-block works.

B. "V" angle chisel (medium) The length of the blade is 15 mm and the length of the handle is 250 mm. Used mostly for scoring patterns, such as fish fins and bird feathers.

C. "V" angle chisel (small) The length of the blade is 10 mm and the length of the handle is 120 mm. Often used to score the eyes of animals and fish.

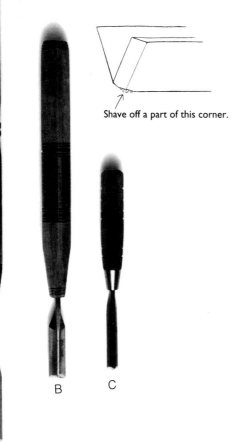

Shave off a part of this corner.

● Flat Chisel

D. Flat chisel (large) Also called a three-*sun* (one *sun* is about 1.19 inches) chisel, the length of the blade is 90 mm and the length of the handle is 550 mm. The thickness of the blade and the chisel's weight are important factors, since this is used for large, multi-block sculptures. Avoid using a chisel with a thin blade, since it will tend to make you tired. Choose one that feels a little bit heavy when holding it. Avoid chisels with round or square handles: octagonal, slightly thick handles, are easier to hold and help conserve your strength. Since the flat chisel is used frequently, its blade tends to become nicked quickly. It is best to own a second large chisel for finishing.

E. Flat chisel (medium) Also called a two-*sun* chisel (2.38 inches), the length of the blade is 60 mm and the length of the handle is 330 mm. This chisel is especially used for medium and small works. Use this chisel following rough shaving with a large, flat chisel.

F. G. Flat chisel (small) These are chisels with 30 mm and 40 mm long blades. (In both cases the handles are 120 mm). Both are used for finishing.

H. Flat chisel (small) The length of the blade is 15 mm and the length of the handle is 150 mm. It also called a "thrusting chisel." It is used to carve holes or to shave narrow places that are difficult to reach with other kinds of chisels.

B   C

A

D   E   F   G   H

"V" angle chisels are used mainly to draw sketches or score patterns. They can create straight, sharp, lines and can leave unique traces by carving with the blade turned to the right or left. The tip of the blade is V shaped, and the common angles of the V are 45°, 60°, 80°, and 90°. The 60° and 80° chisels are used quite often. The 60° chisel is used most of all because it can carve deep and clean.

The point of an "V" angle chisel moves at an acute angle to the ice; thus, cutting with it becomes difficult when it is sharpened. Shave off a part of the corner (refer to the illustration) before using the chisel. Also, the thinner the blade is, the less the resistance from the ice is, and the sharper the carving will be.

Flat chisels are used mainly for rough shaving and for finishing work. Since there is no angle at the tip of the blade, flat chisels can't create many varieties of carving; however, they can give simple images by leaving traces of blade. Since the type of cut is different depending on whether one uses the front or the back, it is important to use both sides of the flat chisel properly. Use the front of the chisel to make the surface of ice completely flat, and use the back to make it round.

I. This is a custom made drill specially ordered from the manufacturer to improve on the electric drill generally available. It has a round bit especially for ice sculpture. In instructions for the works in this book, this is referred to as an electric drill with a round-tipped bit. The rotating edge of the blade can carve a surface round, and it can also carve deep. It gives a softer touch than using gouge chisels, and creates unique reflections when the work is illuminated. I use this drill mainly for carving patterns.

● Electric Drill

● Gouge Chisel

J. Gouge chisel (large) The length of the blade is 100 mm and the length of the handle is 580 mm. This gouge is quarter-rounded. Because they have very little curvature to their blades, these gouge chisels can create subtle touches. They are both used for rough carving of large works and for finishing.

K. Gouge chisel (medium) The length of the blade is 50 mm and the length of the handle is 110 mm. The tip is quarter-rounded. This is the most-used chisel among gouge chisels. Several examples of carving by this chisel are shown in the color photographs: in particular seaweed, women's clothes, and wood grain.

L. Gouge chisel (small) The length of the blade is 25 mm and the length of the handle is 240 mm, with a half-rounded tip. This chisel can carve round and can be used for boring holes.

M. Gouge chisel (small) The length of the blade is 15 mm and the length of the handle is 140 mm. The tip is quarter-rounded. Primarily used to create fish sculpture, especially in carving lines of the eyes, scales, and dorsal fins.

N. Gouge chisel (small) The length of the blade is 10 mm and the length of the handle is 160 mm, with a quarter-rounded tip. Exclusively for scoring the lines of the eyes of fish and birds.

185

Quarter-rounded

Half-rounded

Gouge chisels have a round-tipped blade for carving patterns, and are used for rough carving as well as finishing. There are many kinds of gouge chisels, and each has a different length and a different curve of blade. The terms quarter-rounded and half-rounded describe the curvature of the blades (refer to the above illustration). It is convenient to have many kinds of gouge chisels, since each leaves a different trace according to its particular curvature.

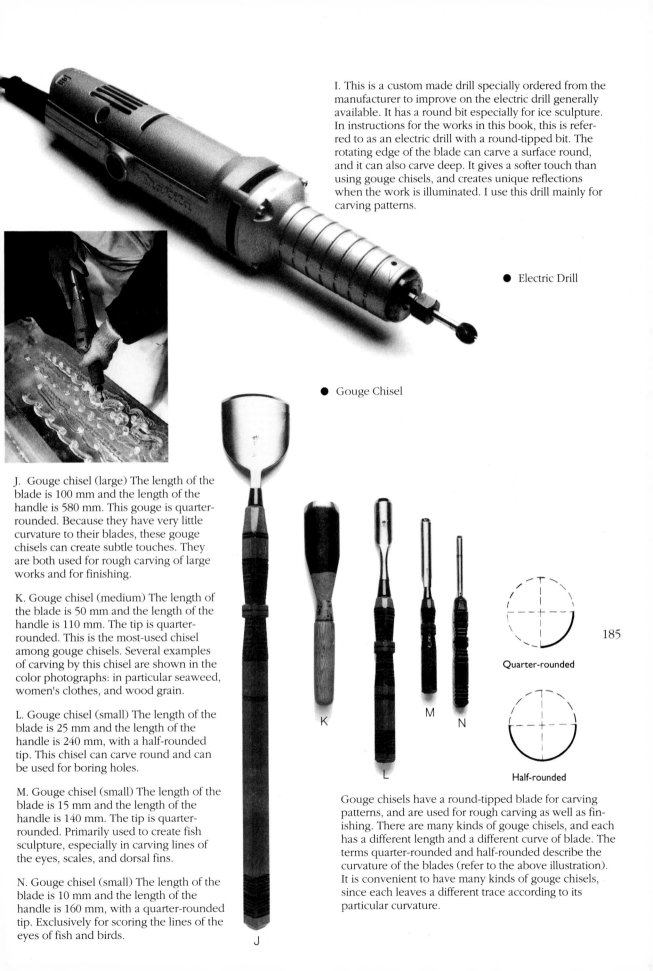

● Saw

Used for cutting ice and for rough carving. In addition, it is used for creating wildness by scoring lines on the surface of works of animals. This is an indispensable tool for joining ice together when piling up ice pieces (see page 189). It is good to train the free hand as well as your whip hand so that both are used to work the saw smoothly.

O. Scroll saw. The length of the blade is 280 mm and the length of the handle is 130 mm. Because its blade edge is fine, the vibration transferred to the ice is minimized. Because of its thin, long shape, the scroll saw is ideal for shaving places where chisels cannot reach.

P. Saw (medium) The length of the blade is 300 mm and the length of the handle is 160 mm. Used when creating works with a quarter or one-fifth of an ice block.

Q. Saw (large) The length of the blade is 480 mm and the length of the handle is 220 mm. Used for multi-block works. Use the large saw to shave off excess ice or for rough carving.

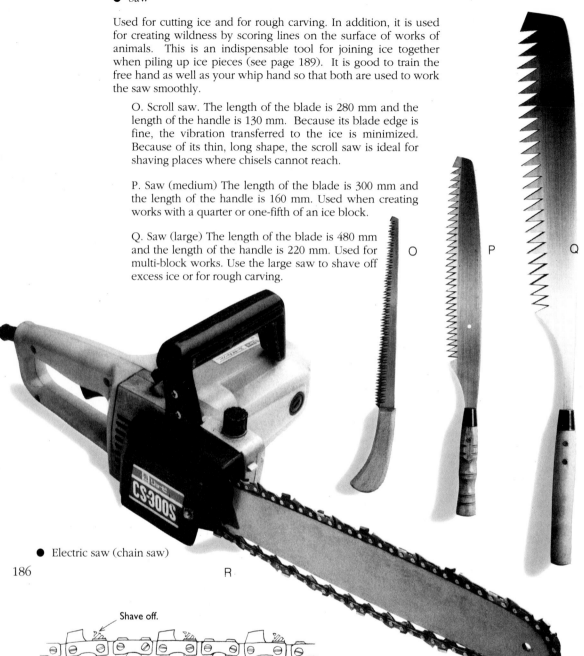

● Electric saw (chain saw)

R

Shave off.

R. Electric saws sold in hardware stores are designed for woodworking; no electric saws made especially for ice carving are available. Before using an electric saw designed for woodworking, it is good to shave off the projections located between the blades with a file or a grinder (refer to the illustration above). By doing so, rotation is improved, the speed and sharpness of the blade are increased, and the tool becomes especially effective in cold areas.

Although electric saws are usually used to cut one block of ice in two, to carve rough, and to bore holes, they are also frequently used to shave off excess areas, since with this type of saw one can give edges to curves where regular saws cannot.

Push the button of the electric saw with the right hand and guide the saw by holding it with the left hand. Here again, the benefits of training both hands are apparent. The basics of using an electric saw are to stand with correct posture and to firmly hold the handle to prevent the edge of the blade from moving left and right. If the chain is slack, it can come off while working and cause serious injuries: it is crucial to inspect the tension of the chain thoroughly before using the saw.

● Compass

● Ice tongs

S

T

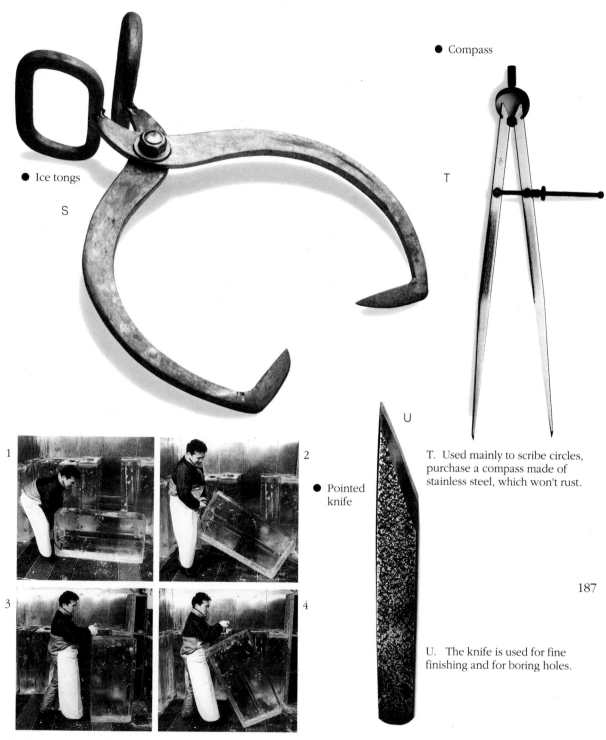

1

2

3

4

● Pointed
knife

U

T. Used mainly to scribe circles, purchase a compass made of stainless steel, which won't rust.

187

U. The knife is used for fine finishing and for boring holes.

S. These tongs are designed for carrying ice and piling ice blocks. Ice that is too big for one person to handle is carried by two people. For this purpose, then, it is best to have two sets of tongs.

It is important to inspect the tongs well before use. If the points are dull, the tongs could easily slip from the ice, causing an injury. When standing ice using tongs, grip at the bottom part of the block (photograph 1), and raise straight up (photograph 2), upending it. Be sure

that both points of the tongs firmly grip the same position on each side of the ice before attempting to lift it. When laying ice blocks down, place the tongs near the top corner of the ice (photograph 3) and bring the block down toward you. When the ice leans at about 60°, immediately lift the tong handles to the top side (this is called turning the tongs) (photograph 4) and lay the ice down.

BASIC TECHNIQUE

Although there are several basics in ice carving, here I will explain essential technique that has to be mastered.

● Joined ice

There are two methods of assembling ice sculptures; one is piling several ice blocks onto one ice block (100 cm x 55 cm x 25 cm) before starting carving, and the other is carving each part first and then assembling them. Both methods are called *joining*, or assembling, ice. The important point in both methods is gluing. To do this, it is essential that the surfaces to be glued are flat and that the flat ice is glued with the technique of joining ice using a saw.

Making the Surface Flat

One of the basics is to first make the four edges level and then to make the surface level according to the edges, irrespective of the size of the ice. It is better for beginners to start by drawing the size needed on the ice using a ruler and shaving along these guidemarks with a chisel. Use this method not only for the purpose of joining ice using a saw, but also for works that first require flat ice. Perform this leveling with the ice at waist height, placing the ice on a wooden stand that won't slip.

Place the front of a flat chisel parallel with the ice (photograph 1). Hold and guide the end of the handle of the chisel with the right hand. Place the left hand on the chisel slightly below halfway (photograph 2).

After shaving around the four edges (photographs 3 and 4), vigorously shave off the center part, leaving it higher than the edges (photographs 5 and 6).

1

188

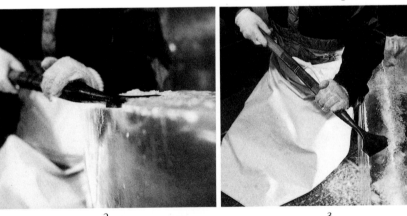

2   3

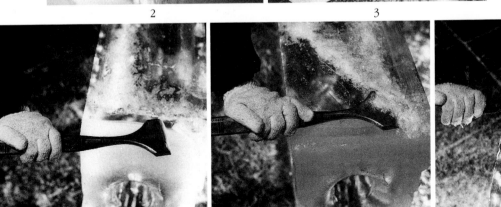

4   5   6

Joining Ice Using a Saw

A method called joining ice using a saw is employed to connect ice together. This technique keeps ice both level and safe when gluing piled ice blocks together. The tricks for this method are to use the forward two-thirds of the saw blade, to move the saw forward gradually, and to do the work at a height between eye and waist level.

1

- Basic Action

Place the blade of a saw between two stacked ice pieces. Always keep the saw at a right angle to the ice (photograph 1) and move the blade gradually as when cutting wood. Doing this shaves flat the roughness of the top and bottom ice pieces, and they become joined together.

- Correcting Level in Ice

When the ice is not level after the basic movements of joining ice using a saw have been completed, correct it by again using a saw. Place the blade of a saw between the ice peices at the higher side, saw to the center of the ice, and stop. Pull the saw out, turn the blade over, re-insert it, and cut back to the original starting point (photograph 2). This is called turning a saw. Repeat this process until the block is level, then place the blade at either edge and make one final pass between the ice pieces (photograph 3).

2

- When Ice Is Thin

Thin ice is prone to cracking under stress. To reduce the resistance between the ice and the saw as much as possible, run the blade diagonally (photograph 4). Proceed otherwise according to the basic movement.

3

189

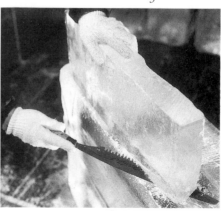

4

The techniques for carving a ball and a straight pole are basic to ice sculpture. In particular, balls become warped as time passes if they are not carved according to standard technique. In addition, size is important: a ball with a diameter of 1 meter is too big. It is important when carving to keep in mind that there is a suitable size for each object. Carve these pieces after studying the correct procedure.

Carving a Ball

Prepare an accurate, perfectly square cube of ice. A large flat chisel tends to make unintentional moves. It is better to use a flat chisel with a blade that is 3 to 4 cm long.

Place the back of a flat chisel at the top center of the ice (photograph 1). Hold the end of the handle of the chisel with the right hand and stretch the right index finger. Place the left hand at the base of the blade and move the chisel forward by steering the chisel with the right hand. Slowly move the chisel around to the center of the adjacent side, leaving a smooth curve (photograph 2). It is wise to use a compass to draw circles on the right and left sides of the ice beforehand and to carve the ice using the drawing as a guide.

Repeat the chiseling and carve the shape of a cross by rotating the ice around (photographs 3, 4, and 5). This cross is the key point. It is important to carve the cross accurately on the center of the ice, to keep the curve radius consistent, and to carve the width of the cross the same as that of the chisel.

Then turn the ice upside down. Carve a cross on this side of the ice in the same way (photographs 6, 7, and 8).

1

2

Next, carve a diagonal line up to the center of an edge, removing a corner (photographs 9 and 10). Shave off the rest of the parts jutting out and complete a half ball (photographs 11, 12, 13, and 14).

Turn the half ball upside down. Since the ball doesn't lie stable, spread towels or other support under the ice to prevent it from slipping. It is essential to be especially careful while carving the back.

Repeat the movements shown in photographs 9 to 14 (photographs 15 and 16). When the sphere is almost done, examine the whole body (photograph 17) and correct any warped areas (photograph 18). Photograph 19 is the finished ball.

9

10

11

192

12

13

14

15

16

17

18

19

Carving a Column

The technique for carving a column is similar to that used for carving a ball.

To make the piece stable enough to stand as a column, leave a small square section on both ends for bases. First, draw circles on both ends using a compass, and then saw into the ice according to the lines (photographs 1 and 2). Keep this circle shape as a guide line in carving the column.

Put the back of the flat chisel on the top surface of the ice and gradually move the chisel forward to the center of the other side of the ice, establishing the roundness of the marked circle with the right hand (photographs 3 and 4). Repeat this movement from end to end. Using the same method, carve the rest of the corners to make them round (photographs 5 and 6).

194

1

2

3

4

5   6

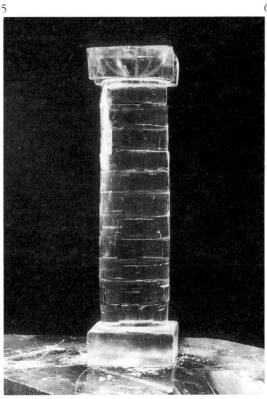

7

After carving the whole piece of ice,
stand the column up (photograph 7) and
check the thickness, balance, and other
elements from a distance, and correct
them as necessary.